The Big Picture

The Seven Step Guide

For Creative Success In Business

A Business Book For Artists

&

Art Book for CEOs

The Big Picture
The Seven Step Guide For Creative Success In Business
The Business Book For Artists
The Art Book For CEOs
by RD Riccoboni
rdriccoboni.com
Copyright ©2012 by RD Riccoboni
All rights reserved, printed in United States of America

Published by Beacon Artworks Corporation
1010 University Avenue, Suite 474, San Diego, CA 92103
Editor, Maryellen Smith at ReinventionQueen.com
Cover Art, February Sunset in San Diego California by RD Riccoboni

No part of this publication may be reproduced or utilized in any form or by any means, electronic, or mechanical, including photo, digital, recording, or by any information storage and retrieval system without permission from the author and publisher, except by a reviewer who wishes to quote brief passages of 300 words or less in conjunction with a review written for inclusion in a magazine, newspaper or broadcast which credits the artist and author. RD Riccoboni®

The author of this book does not dispense medical advice or prescribe the use of any technique as a form of treatment for physical, emotional or medical problems without the advice of a physician either directly or indirectly. The intent of the author is only to offer information of a general nature to help you in your quest for emotional and spiritual well being. In the event you use or do not use any information in this book which is your constitutional right, the author and the publisher assume no responsibility for your actions.

ISBN: 978-0-9850931-2-9

First Printing, First Edition
Manufactured in The United States Of America
https://www.createspace.com/3839389 (for copies of book)

To my mom

for letting me get in her paint by numbers set

when I was four years old

With Gratitude and Appreciation

I would like to thank the following persons and organizations for support:

Paul O'Sullivan for suggesting I write this book after we had lunch and talked about the seven studios and wrote them down on a napkin at Casa de Reyes.

Connie Stewart for energetic friendship and wisdom.

Kathleen Reinhardt, for vision that astounds all of us.

Nancy Berger, my insightful buddy who is always there at the right time and moment.

Peggy McColl, my friend, mentor and teacher who inspired me to realize it absolutely could be done.

Maryellen Smith, my editor who was a breeze to work with.

Tanya Stockton, my publisher at Publishing Unleashed.

Jayne Moffitt, my good friend and co-creative artist and business wiz extraordinaire.

Dave and Dolly Riccoboni, my parents who always supported my artist dreams.

Katie Cubeta, my High School teacher and mentor whose guidance ignited the inner artist.

Richard Long, my art teacher at Joel Barlow High school In Redding Connecticut who taught me not to make mud with my paints.

Gail and Chuck Ross and Joe Kates, believers in everything we do with amazing cooperation and artistry at Fiesta de Reyes in beautiful Old Town San Diego State Historic Park..

Bruce and Alana Coons, whose leadership at SOHO, (Save Our Heritage Organization) has preserved of many San Diego landmarks the world loves and has inspired many of my paintings today.

My friend Robb Drury, for brainstorming marketing and business saavy.

Rayme Sciaroni, musical artist extraordinaire and friend.

Charles Reidelbach, for a great passion for art, legal consul and friendship over the years that has seen me from the beginning thoughts of many projects.

Catherine Carlson, for financial advice and friendship.

Linda Goodman, for guidance in showing me the correct way to set up a business.

Bob Proctor, for mentoring and an Insight of The Day

Bonnie Druschel, for great feedback from an amazing artist.

Patricia Fimbres, for dedication at Beacon Artworks and the courage to grow as an artist.

Larry Hanberg, for making a positive impact in our presentations with the expertise of a true artist and bringing amazing snacks to the table for us to enjoy!

Christie Conochalla, for dedication and a love of reaching for the artist you are.

David Hockney, for igniting a brilliant passion and courage to be myself when I saw his glorious paintings.

Beacon Artworks Gallery, for an amazing showcase for all of us!

My collectors, customers, students and patrons who have supported
my art career from day one without you this could not be.

Old Town San Diego State Historic Park & California Parks for the opportunity of a lifetime and the support to showcase San Diego to the world and having art be part of that.

To friends and family who have passed and believed and inspired, angels everyone!

Rick Hoffman, Paul Cadmus, Anna Hyatt Huntington, Maria Riccoboni Nordlund, Keith Haring, Debbie Chambers & My art teacher in Elementary and Middle school Mr. Richard Lavine

Contents

Foreword by Peggy McColl xi
Introduction xiii
A message from the author xv

CHAPTER ONE
How you Paint The Big Picture.. 3

CHAPTER TWO
You Paint The Big Picture by Owning it First 7

CHAPTER THREE
Take Charge of your Dreams - Be the Boss of Your Destiny 15

CHAPTER FOUR
Share What You Love to Do – Telling is Selling 24

CHAPTER FIVE
Thinking your Big Picture Correctly 33

CHAPTER SIX
Be Aware of Your Fears and Turning Them Around 43

CHAPTER SEVEN
Switch Failure Into Opportunity 53

CHAPTER EIGHT
Love Yourself and Others 58

CHAPTER NINE
Turn A Failure into Opportunity and Discover Your Goldmine 68

CHAPTER TEN
Art Appreciation 73

CHAPTER ELEVEN
Knowing What Other People Want The Art of Hearing and Listening................ 82

CHAPTER TWELVE
Nurture your Spirit by Clearing your Clouded Mind 89

CHAPTER THIRTEEN
Magnetize What You Want 96

CHAPTER FOUTEEN
Having Fun with Having Fun - Co-create a Future with Others! 102

CHAPTER FIFTEEN
Take a Y.O.U. Turn 106

CHAPTER SIXTEEN
Affirmation and Emotion Feeling 115

CHAPTER SEVENTEEN
See Yourself in The Big Picture 119

CHAPTER EIGHTEEN
Tap into Your Power and the Magnificent Power of the Universe 123

CHAPTER NINETEEN
Asking 127

CHAPTER TWENTY
Wake Up and Dream 135

CHAPTER TWENTY ONE
Make Space 145

CHAPTER TWENTY TWO
Set the Stage 148

CHAPTER TWENTY-THREE
Make a Big "To Do" Over Tomorrow 153

CHAPTER TWENTY-FOUR
Discipline the Fun Way 159

CHAPTER TWENTY FIVE
Contribute Support with Your Highest Level of Permission 167

CHAPTER TWENTY-SIX
Goal Setting 171

CHAPTER TWENTY-SEVEN
Keep Track of Your Successes 174

CHAPTER TWENTY-EIGHT
Invest in Your Talent to Find Your Calling 177

CHAPTER TWENTY-NINE
Get Up With The Chickens 185

CHAPTER THIRTY
Find a Niche You Can Scratch 187

CHAPTER THIRTY-ONE
Be a Doorway 190

About the Author 199

Biographical Highlights 201

Foreword by Peggy McColl

Originally Randy called this book The Big Picture for Artists, and you would think that a book called The Big Picture for Artists would only be applicable to … well, artists, right? Well, as it turns out I was completely and pleasantly surprised to find this book is inspiring and packed full of phenomenal wisdom for ANYONE (whether you are an artist or not).

If it were up to me, I'd change the title of this book to The Big Picture and remove the words "For Artists". This book is truly applicable to any one in any type of career or business! And, as things turned out, Randy did change the title of this book and now it is called The Big Picture - The Seven Step Guide For Creative Success In Business.

Randy is considered a mentor to many artists and entrepreneurs who have a desire to pursue their passion and enjoy a healthy and abundant lifestyle as a result. I would consider Randy one of the world's greatest mentors because he understands what it takes to succeed. He's studied success, applied the principles and experiences the just rewards.

Over the years I've had great mentors and I invested in them because they had achieved great results, and I knew I could benefit from their experience. Besides a mentor can shave off years of time and potentially save you thousands of dollars. And, since Randy has invested years of his time and thousands of his dollars in learning and applying proven techniques for success, he has decided to share them with you with this precious jewel you are holding in your hands.

Randy will take you by the hand and walk you through practical and powerful exercises on each and every page.

The structure of this book is brilliant and simple. Following Randy's suggestions is easy which is precisely the way success is meant to be … easy! This isn't complicated. As a matter of fact, Randy suggests you have fun with this and he is absolutely right. When you are in a relaxed state (the state you are in when you are having fun) you are manifesting at an accelerated rate. My advice to you is dig into this masterpiece and follow Randy's guidance and it is with certainty that you will meet with success.

Peggy McColl
New York Times Best Selling Author of *Your Destiny Switch*

Introduction

What if you had a personal invitation to spend an hour, portion of the day, week or month with one of America's most successful artists who is also the CEO of a successful business? Would you have the COURAGE TO SHOW UP for such a wisdom filled opportunity?

In **The Big Picture** - *For Creative Success In Business* you are invited to partake in that very opportunity; to see and learn how to apply your talent, education, passion, expertise and craft into a profitable career.

Whether you're a budding or an accomplished artist, inspiration and vision is not enough. Giving of your time and talent are not enough, expecting people to want what you have is not enough, doing the footwork is not enough and even on-going action is not enough to get the Big Picture of what you want in Art and Business. After all, the business of art is an art itself!

Within the book are seven workshop sections called "**Studio's**", designed to assist you on your journey. The following exercises are designed to help the creative person to stay grounded and focused in the positive vision desired. Learning to apply techniques and lessons written out here are key ingredients to the secret to success.

The Big Picture - *For Creative Success In Business* will assist you in creating a focused outline for boosting success as well as a self-check in of your progress while learning new dream accountability skills.

This book is a tool kit of sorts with suggestions to reconnect to you to your art career and answer this all important question: "What did I set out to accomplish with my talent?" These suggestions are not meant to replace any other path, medical advice, professional therapy or workshop. They are merely suggestions that have worked for the author, other artists and creative people.

Whether you are an artist or not learning how to effectively use your creativity, product and service to make a living for yourself, benefit and clients are some of the gifts you can discover as you identify and attract your perfect art business customer / opportunity.

You will learn how to keep things in perspective, make smart decision action plans with goals and create manageable daily strategies.

Begin right now to evaluate your journey and see if you are indeed on course creating your Big Picture or just bulls!*##ing yourself. Use the pertinent information inside for your own unique and resonating clear vision, artistic purpose and feel good about creativity in your career!

The Big Picture - *For Creative Success In Business* will jumpstart you onto the thriving road of the thriving artist's life.

A message from the author

My name is RD Riccoboni I am an accomplished artist, best-selling author and founder of a successful art based business. I'm known to some people as The Art Traveler, as I truly love to travel while painting historic landmarks, places, events and people. Every year over 1 million people come to Old Town San Diego State Historic Park to view my paintings in the art studio and gallery I founded. They don't just visit either, they buy art.

Through strangely tumultuous financial times my art business has always thrived. Economic turmoil all around me, yet my business grows. In any economy, especially for an artist, how is this possible? After all, this is art and I am an artist. Aren't artists supposed to struggle? Not to become famous until after they die starving? To that I answer, NO! Not unless the artist wants it to be that way. Anyway, after you're gone it's too late.

What you do with your talent NOW is what matters. I have never known of or attended the funeral of an individual who starved to death because he/she was an artist. Have you? If so, you have my condolences. Do a Google search of "Starving Artist" and you will be appalled at the results and how ingrained this 'story' has become in our cultural thinking.

So how does one accomplish success and make a good living, too? A self-taught artist with no formal art or writing training, yet my art hangs in prestigious collections and affords me and the people who support my business a handsome living. What is going on here?

Here's what's going on. This is what works for me, try it if you like. I take what I love to do, make a decision, apply common sense and value, research, work, create a system then turn it into my business, and repeat it making me an art-preneur, creating a new economy for myself and others.

I did not always know this successful process and when I did learn of it I wasn't sure how to work with it. Let me tell you a bit about my background.

When I was four years old, I discovered my mother's paint-by-numbers set. It was a sailing scene of the tall ship Old Ironsides – the U.S.S. Constitution. One day when no one was looking I got in the paints and completed the picture! I was off and running, painting and drawing everything around me. In school, my favorite subjects quickly became Show and Tell and Art class. My parents were supportive of my artistic abilities, as it kept me quiet for hours. One day, my aunt brought me a book on the French Impressionist painters. I immediately started copying pictures from the book, happily making my own versions as gifts for my family. I boldly told everyone, "When I grow up, I'm going to be an artist!"

Artists often receive negative input from outside influences – well-meaning people who are stuck in the emotions of lack and drama. I was no exception. How many times have you heard the phrase "starving artist" or heard someone say, "An artist isn't taken seriously until he's dead"? After all, that was life of an artist – struggle and sacrifice for art's sake in order to leave a legacy for the world, discovered and revered long after the fact.

Over the years, waves of success came and went for me. I could never quite put my finger on why this happened. What caused it? It certainly could not be me! Perhaps it was the economy or the fashion of the time. Perhaps certain colors were in and others were out. It had to be an uncontrollable source outside of me, right? I seemed to be always swimming against the tide.

A "Real" Job

Before long, as so many other budding artists do, I left the idea of being an artist behind. One day a distant relative had said to me, "An artist? That's crazy talk. Get a real job, be a banker – that's what your cousin is." Before I knew it, I was a banker, followed by careers in retail and human resources, with the thought of being an artist always haunting me in the pit of my stomach.

At work, my coworkers saw the gift I had, but I had lost sight of it through negative thinking. I'd be fuming to myself while decorating the company bulletin board, Oh if people just knew what a wonderful artist I really was, I could leave this awful job; I'd show them! Thriving on my inner drama, I never even heard the positive comments they said.

In the late 1980s my family and I had some serious financial mishaps. Bitter, disillusioned, and barely making ends meet, one day I received a solicitation from a large nonprofit asking for money for AIDS research, and it sent me over the edge. I wanted desperately to help and did not know how. You see at the time, I had lost my complete circle of close friends, and some coworkers because of this terrible disease. Those were bleak days. Upon opening the letter, I thought, I am so sick and tired of this dis-ease, I have no money.... What could I possibly do? This little voice inside me said, "Paint, you can paint!" and that's exactly what I did. I got into action and began painting. This decision was a defining moment in my life. I started creating enough paintings for an exhibit with happy, upbeat, bright colors. I rediscovered myself and began sharing my art with others.

"You Can Paint!"

Soon word was out that I was an "artist." A wonderful man, Brien offered his lovely home as a gallery for our fundraiser. We found more artists who wanted to be involved, it became a group art exhibition, and we selected a worthy foundation. We invited every person we knew, and it was a huge success! I discovered right then and there that I wanted to be a painter and assist others by using my talents.

I moved cross-country to California and continued to do work as an artist. Eventually I was represented by a world-class art museum, and a book of my artwork, Rainbow Nation, was published internationally.

I have traveled all around the country, making many friends, showing art, signing books and meeting young artists who wanted to be like me someday! I've launched more shows, and I've served on the boards of local art organizations. One of the exhibits was recognized by the White House, and involved traveling to Washington, D.C., to show how art can bring awareness and community together on important healthcare issues.

However, I didn't continue to develop new goals and practice the positive thought processes I had stumbled upon. Without the proper tools to keep me going, I stalled. I bought back into the negative, "woe is me," poisonous thinking around me. Like a worn-out tire, eventually I blew out...literally. A physical injury threatened to end my career abruptly, which would cause me to become that suffering artist everyone warned me about! I required and desired a miracle!

Needing inspiration, I took myself to the bookstore. In the architecture section, I heard that familiar voice within tell me, "You can paint flowers," so off to the gardening section I went. Upon arriving there, BAM!, a book literally fell off the shelf and hit me in the head, landing right side up at my feet. The book was The Artist's Way by Julia Cameron, and it was the catalyst that got me back on track.

Attracting the Positive

I finally realized that I had to change my thinking! Because of my thoughts, I was attracting both negative and positive circumstances. Not knowing how to change, once again fate would have its way. A friend recommended the book Healing Back Pain by Dr. John E. Sarno, which gave me another concrete, powerful tool.

Putting little sticky notes around my house, car, and everywhere, I began telling myself that I was a healthy, happy artist; that what I do is draw and paint. I made affirmations and stick figure drawings on them of what I wanted in life. Not realizing that I was affirming and visualizing, I began to see myself healing, creating beautiful art, surrounded by loving, appreciative friends and family, living abundantly with people from all over who enjoyed my creativity. I imagined how that would feel, and that is how it really feels, because it is the very life I live today. I took notes of what worked and took charge of rediscovering myself and my destiny.

With practice, an amazing shift in my thinking has occurred, along with the folks I'm attracting into my life. It's actually become difficult to have negative thoughts, and I am so grateful for that! One thing I have come to realize about changing my thinking habits is that even if I don't get it at first, it will eventually get me! These tools are what I share with you in the Big Picture.

These days, setting goals, taking action and following through to reach them allows me to live a full life surrounded by wonderful, loving friends. I have my own business. I've opened a respected art gallery. I'm a published artist and author whose work is exhibited in business establishments and museum spaces. I share my story with groups of students, business professionals, and charitable organizations. Once again, that little boy is running around showing his pictures and telling stories!

What I have come to learn is we're never done, retired, or graduated, and that's what keeps life exciting! Joy is the success in the journey of life, not material things. You will attract those outside things – money, stuff, relationships – when you are joyous. Keeping our side of the street clean on this journey and inspiring others to reveal their success promotes more joy and more miracles. I have seen it in my own life and in the lives of others.

You can accomplish your desires and intentions with right thinking, self-responsibility, and right actions. You too can experience miracles, find your purpose and passion, and joyfully be drawn to success.

What am I in the business of? That's easy you may say, "Art. You're an artist, you paint and sell pictures." That is incorrect. That is only an aspect of my business.

Whether making art and selling it or sitting in a cubicle pushing paper, answering the phone, serving food, running someone's else's office,. I am in the same business. If I don't believe in what I am doing that business will suffer or fail. It is something I call The Big Picture. How we see ourselves or don't see ourselves is The Big Picture which links us all together. A Big Picture stretches and expands you. It doesn't matter if you're an artist, we are all in the same business, The Big Picture Business. You see, we make symbols or pictures in our minds first with thoughts and express those pictures in words to others.

What we BELIEVE and DO with those "Picture Thoughts" is what connects to - or separates us from - our desired outcome.

Your current personal or collective artist life situations come down to one thing. You either believe and are in love with what you are doing, telling that to others or doing that work and not liking it one bit. You are either happy or you're unhappy. You're either selling the greatest thing since sliced bread or selling a load of crap. If you have a lot of drive and belief, you might be doing both and very well, at that. There can be two answers to everything. There is plenty of thriving mediocre talent out in the world simply because of drive and hard work. There are plenty of talented artists who are genius at their craft yet lazy when it comes to work. They seem to love to complain about their mediocre life…blah, blah, blah.

I will be honest here. I'm not going to hold your hand throughout this book. You are going to have to learn to do that yourself. However, I will share what I have come to know and that is, Success all begins with YOU! Beginning with the story you tell others and what you believe about your own story has everything to do with your accomplishments. I am not speaking of money; I am speaking of sharing sincere abundance with love. More importantly, what "picture" are you selling back to yourself? Are you expressing your individuality in thoughtful, loving and prosperous ways? Where is what you express taking you and others? Is your life enriched? What are you physically doing with your talents? Does the service you provide enrich your life and the lives of others with value? These are serious questions that only you can answer. Rest assured that no matter how you answer these questions, your world will change.

In the following pages I share with you suggestions and the very same creative methods, perspectives and techniques that I use to create my personal and business success, things I have kept track of over the years; procedures that worked through many challenging situations for many of my friends and myself.

I would never suggest anything that I have not personally tried myself. If you apply just one exercise, it could change your life when you apply it consistently, then you will have mastered it. I still do them, as do my teachers, friends and people I mentor and our lives continue to get better and better.

Please tailor any one of these ideas to your specific needs. Begin with a vision of your Big Picture, add some direction and purpose applied with love and you will end up with a Big, Big, Big Picture or something even better. Why? Because you're evolving. When you come from love, the more it works. The more you believe in what you're doing the more you know it pays to be an artist!

Best wishes to you on your road to a happy artistic and prosperous destiny. If you can lovingly imagine and feel what you want it means it already exists.

May your creative success in business and life astonish you!

RD "Randy" Riccoboni.

Artist (merriam-webster.com)

noun

1. a person who produces works in any of the arts that are primarily subject to aesthetic criteria.

2. a person who practices one of the fine arts, especially a painter or sculptor.

3. a person whose trade or profession requires a knowledge of design, drawing, painting, etc.: *a commercial artist.*

4. a person who works in one of the performing arts, as an actor, musician, or singer; a public performer: *a mime artist; an artist of the dance.*

5. a person whose work exhibits exceptional skill.

EXPAND

6. a person who is expert at trickery or deceit: *He's an artist with cards.*

7. *Obsolete.* an artisan.

Creative

adjective

1: marked by the ability or power to create : given to creating <the *creative* impulse>

2: having the quality of something created rather than imitated : IMAGINATIVE <the *creative* arts>

3: managed so as to get around legal or conventional limits <*creative* financing>; *also*: deceptively arranged so as to conceal or defraud <*creative* accounting>

CREATOR

noun

one that creates usually by bringing something new or original into being; *especially capitalized*: GOD 1

The Big Picture

The Seven Step Guide

For Creative Success In Business

A Business Book For Artists

&

Art Book for CEOs

RD Riccoboni

Beacon Artworks Corporation
San Diego, California

STUDIO ONE
Take Ownership of the Big Picture

Step One: Beckon Inner Genius.

"When you have to make a choice and don't make it, that is in itself a choice."
—*William James*

In Studio One chapters we will explore integrity-based decision making, focusing on solutions, moving into action and innovate with our creativity.

CHAPTER ONE

How you Paint The Big Picture

This book is a celebration book. A celebration of what you love to do. You're invited to take a journey through these pages. Begin from your current position, which is a direct result of everything that's happened to you. Accept and celebrate this, and realize that if you can change just one thing, one belief or thought, you can change everything. You are that powerful.

I know these techniques work first-hand because they have helped me double my income in just one year. After having many artists come up to me wondering how they could do the same for themselves, I thought: *"Why not write a book?"*

I have seen colleagues, associates and friends who have also achieved phenomenal successes using the principles here in The Big Picture. Some of these successes happened in a short amount of time, while others took longer. How you apply these principles is up to you. I suggest that in addition to reading this book, you apply the exercises at the end of each chapter, called *Studio Play Sheets*. Even better, share and do them with a friend or two and hold each other accountable. Also, you will need some quiet time and tools: a pencil or pen and blank notepad or notebook. I like spiral bound paper to keep my notes organized and easy to find. This is a hands-on studio art class where you get to be both the artist and the teacher. As you do the work, you'll have opportunities to step back, take breathers and watch the Big Picture unfold in front of you.

This book is not about finding fame; it is about drawing success to you. Success and fame are two very different things. Success will sneak up on you quietly. Fame, on the other hand, is not what this book is about. Fame is noisy, brash, fickle and embarrassing; it is so much less personal and rewarding. Success hangs around; it is always there for you to tap into it naturally, quietly awaiting your signal. Fame may get you on the evening news; success, on the other hand, will carry you through life toward the end result of what you see as your Big Picture. Success, like art, means different things to different people. No two people are alike and neither are two successes or art expressions. However, success seems to be in everyone's Big Picture and like an art piece you own in your home, gallery or museum, the Big Picture you experience and generate creates a life of emotions and feelings.

There are key ways to create the Big Picture of your success. These things have been proven over time and are simple and easy to use. The way that you discover your success may be different from others but how you apply the discovery is always the same. These key ways require ongoing decision-making, contentment with that decision, a call to action, work, dedication, patience, gratitude and open mindedness.

A strong commitment to the process of getting where you want to be and feeling great about making a living with your art is mandatory. You must be emotionally committed to the process of success and feel good about it deep inside. It is your inner drive, not merely sheer talent that will deliver your success as an artist. To get to where you want to be, as the end result of the thing you desire, you must love the feeling of what it is you are doing. Audacity may deliver fleeting fame; success, on the other hand, is always there with you.

Finally, you alone must accept responsibility for your own expression of individuality. No one else but you can do this work for you. You are the one in charge of your success and your own personal art collection of Big Pictures. Own it. Love It. Be It.

Think of this book as your Big Picture Kit, Toolbox or "Paint by Numbers" set to create dynamic artistry in your life. Inside your kit are exercises that attract success to you in many different ways. Along the way you will learn to honor your time, value and worth. By using the key suggestions in your Big Picture Kit, you'll begin to attract success and abundance into your life.

To make sure you have fun, use the play sheets to dream and wonder. By building up your innocent child-like faith, you will find your niche and gold mine.

The Studio Play Sheet exercises in this book are fun and challenging and will help you tap into your natural ability. The suggested exercises will assist you in tapping into your own inner master artistry of guidance and wisdom. Followed by Creative Activity Points (CAPs) : Career Action Points which, when used, separates serious artists (who are really making a living with their artistry) from the crowd. Share this book with other creative folks, too. Offer assistance and guidance to others when appropriate and have lots of fun doing so. As your light begins to shine brighter and brighter, others will subconsciously be alerted and want to know what is up with you. Share your insights; you might just be the best teacher another artist could have. The best gift you can give to others is to follow your passionate heart's desires and model your own life working well. So, have fun because you ARE naturally fun and you can impact the world!

You are ultimately responsible for fulfilling your purpose and happiness. Enjoy and use the exercises as your own. Eventually you may develop your own exercises allowing you to gain new insights along the way. Create your own joyful processes as your art career grows. When you enjoy the journey as much as the goals and the destinations, you will experience and appreciate the artist full-to-the-brim life. At times, you may find some of my suggestions to be repetitive. Hang in there; this is how we learn. Study and re-study these exercises. Read other books that relate to these topics and then read them again.

You have this book in your hand and it's a great place to start!

We all start somewhere with great intentions. As little children we have aspirations and I did and am sure you did as well. Everything looked bright and full of possibility. When I was a little boy, I heard positive questions and statements like, "What do you want to do or be when you grow up? Keep your eye on the prize. Do your best work and keep at it." I also heard negative questions and statements like, "Who do you think you are? That lifestyle is not for you; that is for them. You are too nice; You'll never get ahead. Money doesn't grow on trees. Artists don't make money or get any recognition till they're dead. Oh yes, that's what rich people do but you're not one of them. We are not rich. Thinking is dangerous. You should never want what they have; That's a sin. You get a job, go to work, pay your bills and die; that's life. Get real!" Sound familiar?

How ridiculous! What a lousy Big Picture that paints in little minds! No wonder people wind up feeling screwed up, having to go through years of therapy, working at unhappy jobs and hanging around people they don't want to be with. They might take medication, drink, and eat excessively to escape and just get through the day! It's the artist soul that is starving to death from all the "good" advice they pick up and begin to believe along the way.

As a teenager and like so many other young folks my age, I was miserable in my own skin, so frustrated I was ready to pop out of it! Everything I heard and saw seemed contrary and hypocritical. Whenever I questioned anything about it I was punished. Eventually I lost my self-permission to dream at all as a result of well-intentioned grown-ups. I withdrew into a world of drawing pictures, keeping quiet and staying out of sight. It is amazing what little ears pick up along the way from disenchanted adults. Thank God I had an "ah ha" moment back then and saw through some of the double standards around me. However, I also knew I would have to bide my time until I was old enough to be on my own. In the meantime, I listened and looked for the good stuff. Painted in my mind were glimmers of hope on my road to the Big Picture of freedom and success. The Good Stuff. What is the Good Stuff? It is the positive aspects of that big picture I created by putting all the exciting, exhilarating possibilities in my thoughts and into my heart that would one day materialized into reality one day.

Most artists get very upset when people label them or call their art or work "stuff". I love it when they do! Especially when they say," I love your stuff" or "This is really good stuff." *Yes*, I say to myself, *my secret label of success is to love and appreciate the good stuff I create.* Next I take a moment to feel grateful that I am able to craft the stuff in the first place!

Nowadays I have fun and am still on an exciting journey every day. While I don't claim to know everything, I certainly have a good time exploring further enhancement of my expertise. I firmly believe we can tap into the universal energy that "knows" everything. When we tap into that our artistry is born. It is how we become confident and successful.

Being an artist at heart is like being a quiet rebel. I like to observe, learn and then create new things from my observations. Observation is a key ingredient in the success of your Big Picture. Creating new ideas and acting on them are yet more vital ingredients. Then, like a kid in an elementary school play, you allow yourself to participate in your very own "show and tell." Nearly every day I am asked, "How did you do this? How did you become successful?" I share my experiences and tell them the same things you will read about in this book.

DO - BE

As far as the business of art and making a living in art, I have found that when you create what you love, the income comes. When you focus on the income first, it just doesn't work. It is almost as if some sort of invisible barricade prevents it from coming. So, DO and BE what you love, love what you do, be and do it for the enrichment of others and enjoy. In other words, live in joy – art brings joy - you are in the business of joy – mind your business! I can't drive this point home enough. When people look for work often times they have no passion or even knowledge of what they see. They just walk into a place of business blindly looking for a paycheck and then wonder why they don't get called back for an interview. At least one person per day solicits our gallery with literally no idea that they are in an art gallery to begin with! Please, DON'T DO THIS even if you are in survival mode, desperately needing income. DO seek work that supports your inner drive and passion. DO be aware and know where you are; this way you benefit both yourself and your employer. By first identifying what makes you tick, you ignite your drive, which is essential for success. Humor helps too, so be easy about all this stuff and laugh at yourself. Remember this- Joy, Fun, Laughter and Love create the best Big Picture.

Utilizing your natural talents is the best way to make a living as an artist. What are your talents? The Big Picture is going to help you investigate and recognize what you are naturally good at. Spend time investigating, experimenting and discovering doing what you're naturally good at and you will get to know yourself better along the way.

Before you can turn your talents into strengths, you have to first know what they are. The most successful persons align what they do with their natural abilities. Know yourself, be yourself, and then share what you are good at with others. You'll never have to work at what you don't like doing anymore. Once you recognize your natural talents and start knowing yourself, and start implementing them, the return back will be on seeing the artist you really are not just the art you make.

Your future is now, the stage is set and this is your Big Picture success story. Are you ready to be the person you want to portray to the world? Here we go into Studio One.

CHAPTER TWO

You Paint The Big Picture by Owning it First

We live in a world of mostly negative "monkey see – monkey do" thinking and talking. You do have the power to switch that incoming bombardment of external messages to your own independent thinking and start talking with some courage and confidence.

Science has taught us that everything is energy. When you have creative thought symbols in your mind, manifestations of what you think about are actually symbols of energy. Your art career, your money, bank account, your physical wealth, as well as the lack of it are all manifested symbols, evidence of energy. Energy is always there and available to tap into with your creative thinking and actions. You will work with creating symbols all through the Big Picture. You will learn that the symbols that you create magnetize your personal evidence of abundance -or the lack of it. Take ownership of your art career by creating symbols that show the Universe that you are serious by your intention. This provides clarity, which helps you focus on the solutions that create your desired outcome.

People believe in different wealth symbols based on what they think they deserve and what their level of comfort is. This relates to the artistic creations right down to the customer buying the art. People individually generate prosperity consciousness and create symbols in their minds regarding art and its value.

All tangible goods or services are symbols of energy manifested from creativity and thought Money, as currency, is a symbol of prosperity; we reward one another with money to acquire art. Art is certainly considered an energetic and physical symbol of prosperity and joy.

Some people only collect original art, some signed art editions, some prints, others perhaps only posters. What makes one person feel wealthy may not do it for another person. People will purchase different types of symbols of energy. Though each one of those persons acquired a different symbol of status or appreciation, each still feels wealthy in their own certain way. When the artist fails to see their own creative birthright and how their art creates a positive contribution to the world they miss out on the joy, wealth and affluence that is right in front of them theirs to claim.

Artists are especially born with creative and curious minds that have the ability to fashion untold and wondrous journeys. We artists also generate symbols and hang on to some that are not good for us, allowing these unhealthy symbols to become our story. Do not create symbols that contribute to a story that says life needs to be a struggle. Prosperity is everyone's birthright, including the artist.

Time for some Tough Love

Okay, Let's get a few things out of the way. On my business card it says I'm both an artist and a business person. I make art and sell it; I'm not an English scholar nor do I profess to be a wordsmith. Be serious about your artist calling. I'm not your therapist, parent or baby sitter and I'm going to lay some tough art love out on the table right now. You may not like what I'm about to say. I don't care; this is important. Here goes- There are two types of artists. One is an artist who goes into the world with their art and craft, expanding their Big Picture through diligent and ethical systems and sells their work with integrity, adding value to themselves and the world. The other type of artist remains in ongoing art classes, pontificating, philosophizing on technique, over-explaining their processes of interpersonal feelings and woes of struggle in the art world. The difference between the two is one is a professional artist and the other a bullshit artist!

Yes, some B.S. artists make it to galleries and museums but most do not. Who cares! What does matter is YOU and that you commit to making a living with your art. If not now, then WHEN will you step up to the plate? Let the gas out of the victim wind bag and BE YOU, the sincere, simple, courageous and talented artist you are! You have answered the artist's call. I know and you know that we are all more than our business card says. However you are here to learn insight on making a living with your art.

Life is not a Dress Rehearsal

You are talented enough in the making of your art and as the saying goes, the world is chock full of over educated derelicts, which my friend, includes artists. Now is the time to learn the art of selling and making a living at it. Education is important, however if you are serious about going professional, leave the art classes to the beginners and hobbyists. An occasional class may be fun for brush up, but seriously, do not get caught up in the addiction of 'just one more class and I'll be perfect.' You are already perfect the way you are. The thing you won't learn in art class is how to make a living with your art unless you're teaching the class or own the art school. If you must take any more classes take business classes!

But, before you close this book and go running off to business school or yet another art class, let's explore some of your thoughts. We'll start off by asking a few questions. Are you taking a class to move yourself forward or is it really just another distraction to keep you from making a living with your art? Is there something deep inside you are avoiding? DO you need someone guiding you and holding your hand to accomplish something you probably already know how to do but fear? Have you done that thing you wanted to do five years ago? If not, why not? The sun will rise and fall many times, yet there are no guarantees. What are you waiting for? If you don't take any action toward your dreams and goals today and feel good about them, what will you be doing five years from now? What does the artist's life look like to you? Seriously, this is different for everyone; whatever your picture looks like be sure it depicts a thriving, joyous and prosperous life. If artistic success never comes, if you never make a living with your art can you be happy and love your life no matter what?

The Universe Wants to Hand you a Pay Check

What if I told you there are unlimited blank checks waiting for you to do with them what you desire? The only hitch is you have to know some important things about yourself and your talents. What you do with this knowledge and how you apply it is how you will be able access them.

Your talent is that blank check from the Universe. To access the rewards of that gift of talent, whether artistic talent or not, you must follow the things you are passionate about and make you feel good on the inside. Then, you need to channel that energy into a service that is valuable to others. That is your ticket to many types of freedom. The catch? You have to do the work. I can guide you and share stories that may inspire you but YOU still have to do the work. It's time to beckon your inner genius.

While I have your attention, let's do a powerful exercise. You are a living breathing part of the physical Universe that overflows with abundance in perfect harmony. Breathe in and out and feel the abundance of the Universe that keeps you alive. There is a prosperous windfall in that abundant flow that awaits you. Everything in your life can change in a second when you get in touch with the real and deepest, truest artist self.

Get a blank notebook or legal writing pad (I prefer a spiral bound one to keep things organized) and use the following exercises to ignite your success. Open your heart and you will soon learn and identify that the best things in life are available to you and the world is out to do you good.

Ask yourself, "What is my gift?" then ask, "How can I use this gift to serve the world?" Anyone who seeks to find his or her passion in life will surely find it in this way. Be quiet for a few minutes and ask yourself these questions again. You can take all the action in the world, make lists of what to do, contact all the right people, but if you don't feel good about what it is you are doing, you will self-sabotage the Big Picture. You must feel good about what you take ownership of and you must feel good in action about creating it.

Let's do a practice run of a Play sheet. Get your blank note book and pencil or pen, and start using it to write or sketch your notes and inspirations. Across the front write "My Big Picture Book". Use this for all the studio exercises in the Big Picture Book.

Did you ask yourself what are your gifts and natural talents are? List them in your The Big Picture notebook. Before you can use them in business and make a living with them you have to know what they are.

What are your gifts? For example: One of my gifts is playing Show and Tell; I inspire others and use my creativity as well as make a living doing that and I feel good about that!

Now take full credit for your gifts and own them. Across the top of the page(s) where you have written your gifts, write the following statement: "I own and take credit for these gifts I have with love and gratitude."

Next, on a new piece of paper in your book, make a list of all the things you can accomplish with these gifts and on a scale of one (1) to ten (10) rate how much they excite you. Ten is the MOST exciting! (You can have more than TEN.)

Take a breather and review all the things that excite you.

Now, choose the top FIVE most important gifts, the ones that truly excite you. You must feel good about the action you are taking or you will cease journeying. You can always go back and add more to the list, so just focus on these for now.

Write the five gifts out separately on the top of five separate pieces of paper. Now, underneath what you wrote draw a simple picture, image, and symbol, of what each success gift looks like to you. Our mind sees in pictures, which we will discuss later. Stick figures are acceptable, the simpler the better and drawn only by you. This is important and we'll come back to this soon.

You should now have five separate pieces of paper with the name, title of your gift, and a stick figure picture you drew of it below on each page. For example if your are a painter who is also a writer like myself. You could draw a little stick figure holding a paintbrush and at the top of the page write ARTIST or PAINTER, whatever you are comfortable with. On the next sheet you might draw stick figure writing or a simple drawing of pad of paper and a pencil or pen. What is important is you draw a symbol of your gift.

Next, below each picture, describe its gift. Just do it because as you draw and write you are physically and energetically being drawn to success.

How can you use these gifts written and drawn in your handwriting to serve the world? Use a positive statement answer below the picture.

How can you make the world a better place sharing your individuality, your Big Picture? Again write your answer below. When we act on our dreams we automatically make the world a better place because our joyous energy goes out and comes back to us in wonderful ways that we can't begin to imagine. Did you have a dream when you were little of something you were going to do or be when you grew up? Have you discovered a new passion along the way in your journeys that you would like to explore more? Is there something you are curious about?

People lose that childlike purity and simplicity in what they love to do. As they age however they can re-cultivate this. It takes becoming aware and going within yourself to allow your light to shine again. This light never went out; you may have just stopped paying attention to it. Surrounding yourself with people who reflect this vitality can help you embark on this new journey

When it comes to decisions about what you love to do, most people put them off. Procrastination, as well as feeling unworthy and selfish are actually decisions, to stay stuck.

Intention without action is just potential. When you intend to do something, do not be lazy, start following through immediately. Make a decision to move forward and take ownership of your success.

Focus on the solutions that your artist gifts offer to the world and make it a better place. Your artist living thrives when you know this.

Suit up and show up every day for the life of your dreams.

Make a declaration contract with yourself today, right now, sign and date it. A declaration that holds you accountable to study, grow and develop your success and then own up to it.

I,_____ am committed to my journey of self growth, awareness, abundance and success. I know that I am an unlimited being and I agree to investigate my passions, honor and value my worth and gifts from this point on. I make a decision right now to give myself the best life ever and it feels so good! On these pages I will write and allow myself to dream big, be inspired, create my unlimited reality, and choose beliefs that bring me aliveness and growth. I hereby declare that I will speak of success and prosperity in my words and actions as I inspire and share my insights and gifts with others. This is my Big Picture and I am now taking the necessary steps to turn this into my reality.

Signed _____ Date:_____

Chapter Two's Studio Play Sheet

(Use as many separate sheets of paper and blank sticky notes as needed)

If you have a decision to make right now about improving your future success as an artist, such as: going back to school, finding a new job, changing careers or making new friends, etc. state it below.

From your statement above, list all your possible options and choices here which help you. For example if you want to open a business and no nothing about how to do it you might right down "enroll in business class at community college" or "Interview business owners in the field I wish to go in business in". Make sure they are related to your gifts. If you have not listed your gifts and talents, go back and do so now. Taking action is what gets the wheels of the Universe in motion. Use as many sheets of paper as you require. Think BIG; this is your future and your fantasy life at this moment. Only you can begin the process that turns fantasy into reality. Start writing and drawing.

From the above list of gifts, what options feel most joyful and happy to you? Don't worry about how you will accomplish them.

_____

_____

_____

_____

_____

From your joyful, happy list above, make two columns: one column will indicate why you CAN achieve your goals and the other why you CAN'T.

WHY I Can   **WHY I Can't**

_____   _____

_____   _____

Take all the reasons why you CAN'T and turn them into positive affirmations with a reverse statement indicating WHY you can.

(Example: "I can't be an artist because I don't have the skills and everything I make looks messy." Change this to " I am creative and have many skills that I now apply toward fulfilling my artistic and creative dreams. I am a willing and able student and when my creations are messy, so what? These creations are experiments that better my craft. I will now sign up for an art class online or in person."

Remember those stick figure symbols you drew out on your blank paper or sticky notes? Reflect on them for five minutes a day, seeing them as your success gifts. When you think of the things you want, picture the symbol you drew and picture it coming to you like a magnet. Whether you are an artist or not, your mind sees things in pictures then puts them together like a movie.

My Big Picture Summary

From this moment on list all your success and areas where you are creatively strong and the areas where you struggle. Turn the area's where you struggle into positive affirmations by stating the reverse, as above.

Identify negative habits that hinder your joyful creativity and begin to address them. They need to be dropped like a hot potato!

Treat failures as experiments to better your life experience, craft and knowledge. Ask yourself empowering questions in regards to your experiments.

Ponder ideas that will help you create and expand your gifts.

Speak only of your success when you have breakthroughs and joyful moments. Share and celebrate them. Play show and tell like a child.

Write down positive patterns that are developing and new positive insights.

Once you take ownership of having the art career you desire and make decisions that focus on solutions, it is inevitable that you will find a way to make a living with your art. Your intention beckons inner genius.

Once again, your mind sees in pictures. So create the pictures you want in your mind. Next, draw them out in simple stick figures and then quietly reflect on your pictures. You become successful by doing your work and owning your success and feeling good inside about it. That's how you begin to magnetize the Big Picture to you.

Creative Activity Points

The picture of what the artist's life looks like to you is the same one you subconsciously and consciously portray to your customers and vendors. What does your art career symbolize? Portray the one you want!

Dress and present yourself professionally. If you have only one hundred dollars to spend on promotion, keep it simple by spending it on a good shirt or blouse that never goes out of style and get a new haircut. Convey success in the way you present yourself.

The way to achieve success in your art career is to take ownership of your art career with love and honor. Procrastination is the quickest ride to failure's doorstep.

When you apply what you're naturally good at in business you'll never have to work at what you don't like again, because you know who you are. Turn your natural talents into strengths.

No amount of technical training or studying will accelerate the learning process of making a living with your art, or any business for that matter. Example: giving real presentations to real people who are your future customers.

If you must take more classes, take business and marketing classes. Learn to sell and be a businessperson with your art. You are the boss of your career. Get a part time job selling something you LOVE; then apply the same sales skills to making a living with your art.

Co-create with others.

CHAPTER THREE

Take Charge of your Dreams - Be the Boss of Your Destiny

"Getting ahead in a difficult profession requires avid faith in yourself. You must be able to sustain yourself against staggering blows. There is no code of conduct to help beginners. That is why some people with mediocre talent, but with great inner drive, go much further than people with vastly superior talent." —Sophia Loren

When your life is ideal, what exactly are you doing? Think about that Big Picture. When are you living your life to the fullest? Think about that. What are you doing when you do the happy dance? Think about that. What are you doing when you're happy or at peace? Whatever you're doing, do it and think about it, love it, love the feeling of it, love the thought of it. When you see others doing the things you wish to accomplish yourself, love what they do and what they've done; share the joy with them even if you don't know them. It is like when your favorite actor or actress wins the Oscar; it almost feels like you won too. Feel that way for others. With an attitude like this, you will turn your dreams into reality faster. They Won! We won! I Won! YAY!

Get into that place of joy and get that vibration going.

A Little Secret

When you are upset what are you doing? Don't do that. Here's a little secret: our conscious mind is like the general of our army and our subconscious mind is the troops. They take commands from our conscious mind, the general, and obey the general no matter what. Every time you see something, say something or feel something, the general is sending an order to the troops. What kind of messages do you want to feed your troops? Look at things with appreciation and most importantly, love.

Remember, our subconscious mind sees in pictures and on top of that, it never sleeps! So when you say, "I am going to the store," your conscious mind sees you going to the store. When you say, "I'm not going to the store. I can't stand that place!" your subconscious mind sees a picture of you in the store again and it can't differentiate between going and not going. It sees going to the store you dislike in the picture no matter what. Try it right now and see what I mean. Close your eyes. See yourself going to the store. Now say, "I am not going to the store". What do you see in your mind? The store and you are there.

Let's use another example, this time about money. Say to yourself, as you're about to purchase something, "I just love this shirt I hope I don't overdraw my bank account." Your payment overdraws your checking account. How did that happen?! You holler and get so angry and complain about the bank and their ridiculous charges. You can't keep thinking about what you don't want and "not" keep getting what you "don't" want. Or, perhaps you didn't see that one coming! Have you ever had this happen to you?

Here's another big one. Perhaps in relationships something similar is going on as well. You might say to your friends something like, "I can't seem to ever get ahead" or "All I do is date losers." What is happening here is this-you get what you get because your focus is upon those pictures you keep revisiting in your Big Picture book and keep thinking that this time it will be different. Wanted or unwanted, it still shows up. Unfortunately the ugly truth is that you sort of had it coming to you. Here's why:

Let's repeat this. You are the boss, the chief, captain of your ship and crew, admiral of your navy, the general of your troops. Get it? You, your captain, your general, etc. is the conscious part of you shouting out orders. The naval fleet, tribe or troops is the subconscious part of you that obeys your every command and brings forth what you ordered including the victimization some artists live over and over again. This happens through the vibration memo you continually send! These dedicated warriors may return years later in thought form from the ships that you launched or they may never return again, lost at universal sea. Some may return peacefully, undetected and under your radar as you realize you have the exact life you've always wanted. Some may return with untold riches, through synchronicities and opportunities. Yes, the thoughts you send to the subconscious are that powerful.

Captain Your Crew

Since you are the chief commander of your subconscious world, make a decision to follow your passion and address past mistakes. You may have to let go of some of the old pictures in order to be the person who you really are. This will be one of the best decisions you ever make. By knowing your gifts and following your passions, you can let go of negative things from the past, take them out of your story and create, expand, and stretch your goals. It doesn't diminish or erase the past, but just don't keep allowing negative thoughts to creep into your Big Picture book. Don't keep sending the same message. The messages we transmit are also being received by the trillions of cells in our bodies, good or bad they take note of every thought, environment, food source and condition we put on ourselves.

When I catch myself having a hard time letting go of the past, the easiest thing I find to snap out of it is to focus on the present moment I am in and breathe. Next I take notice of what is right around me. Next I imagine what I would like in small increments. I do this little by little and making my statements bigger as I observe and include those things around me. It's almost like playing a game. For example: I may be out for a walk and stuck in the past of something daydreaming uselessly about it and miss the beauty all around. So I catch myself and say to myself "Here I am walking, that is a lovely flower, this is a beautiful day, let me breathe in the delicious air, there is another lovely flower, (and then I expand my statement) to something like: It sure would be nice to have some flowers like that. Perhaps I can plant some flowers like those in a pot or make a little garden to enjoy for myself. Then I keep it going. I may state: "What a lovely day this is and I am so happy and grateful for this walk and all the beauty to take in". I continue observe more and more and expanding the things around me and before you know it I have popped out of the swirling past, bad mood, or somebody taking up room in my thoughts and into the present moment. We will explore this more in the following workshops. What is important is deciding to Captain your journey.

Make a decision to become the top artist expert at what you want and love to do. You do not have to spread yourself thin either. Find the niche market and attached to your creativity because that's where your gold mine is. A niche market is where you concentrate and focus your sales. Wal-Mart has a niche market and while it is a huge corporation their niche is focused in one area of customers and they bring those shoppers products just for them. They have a system for sharing their products with the world as you can do too. At Beacon Artworks the niche market is local and travel customers who want art that depicts our popular city. With my art I created a system that delivers affordable art products to those customers. This book has a niche market too, for driven artists and business persons who want to know where to begin at making a living with their creativity. Find your niche; next, create your system for mining it.

Read books on people that have accomplished things like you want to accomplish. Dream on it, write on it and be thorough in your investigation of it. The alternative is to do nothing, which will get you more of nothing. You deserve to get more of your dreams. After all, only you can go at them with that gusto. Be persistent and be patient. You will be rewarded and although it may not be in the form you were expecting, be open to what you receive or something better.

Other people may want to help you achieve your dreams whether they know you or not - it's true! Let them. Be open to receiving compliments. Have you noticed how people listen for criticism all the time? Yes, criticism is valuable as long as it's constructive; however, if it's the only thing you listen for, it's destructive.

On the other hand, be careful not to become a victim of pride. I've stumbled upon huge and very positive turning points in my career and also experienced big success in sales from constructive criticism.

Applying what you have already learned and love doing is one of the biggest secrets of success. Take what you love to do, do those things, apply these exercises, and see what manifests.

Mistakes are Blessings in Disguise

Mistakes are bound to happen in life. You are NOT your mistakes! Address your mistakes and learn from them, correct them, don't repeat them. Until you can consciously do this, your crew will keep bringing your mistakes to you face-to-face. Your crew cannot step in to help you without clear and direct orders. If your ego is hollering louder than your crew making you feel victimized or unworthy your subconscious crew will continue to deliver the same mistakes until you align with your higher truth and purpose. It may be time to have a serious talk with your ego mind and say, "Knock it off!" Mistakes are how you learn half of life's lessons. Perhaps that's why people sometimes refer to them as blessings in disguise.

I've heard from artists many times how they got ripped off, were never paid, had art stolen or damaged, and on and on and on. Guess what? I've been there too. I accepted all of the bad behavior and promises. I trusted and did business with persons that I should have known better than to trust. If I had followed my initial gut feeling I would have been better off, realizing something wasn't right. Instead, I let my ego stick its greedy nose right into my business and reinforce negative mythical artist stories I heard and bought into along the way.

Instinct vs. Fear

You don't ATTRACT the wrong galleries, business associates or friends first. You ACCEPT the wrong galleries, business situations and friendships first because you bought into the stories that reinforce that this is all you deserve. You attract more of the same because you're used to it and it becomes the norm. That's the message you are sending to your crew. Now they're invested, too, and follow your orders.

What happens is you accept with willful blindness the first venue that comes along, overlooking the flaws in the relationship. You keep focused on the positive because your feelings tell you this is the road to success so this must be acceptable. You are living your dream, you trust them to follow through, yet things don't change. You start believing what's "wrong" with you and your art career is natural and the way life is.

There's nothing wrong with having art as your business career. It's not a dead end career; it's not Murphy's Law. You accepted the negative behaviors of your associations. There are plenty of dysfunctional art venues that lack integrity. Your job as a professional artist is to research first, ask questions second and then make clear agreements. Don't believe everything you hear or see. In fact, don't believe me blindly either. Follow your own instinct and lead with your intuitive artist spirit, not your fear. If business behavior feels unacceptable, you must leave smoothly and quickly with grace. Save yourself a lot of grief and attorney fees. Make a decision not to put up with any type of dramatic abuse.

Common signs of dramatic abuse or red flags could include: Signing a waiver that the gallery or venue is not responsible for your art while it is in their possession. Business carry liability Insurance ones who don't are not acting responsibly. Saying it is okay to leave your art with them and they will write up "something" later and get it to you. Stating never received your correspondence, including, emails, phone messages which you know you sent and left. Asking for personal favors though they do not know you very well is also a huge red flag. Not paying attention to your needs or stories, appearing distracted and uninterested even when you have an appointment. By the way B.S. artists also do this too.

This is worth repeating, do *not* put up with bad behavior. Leave smoothly and quickly with grace and professionalism.

On the flip side, never, ever bad-mouth, degrade, or insult the venue or persons in which you've had a bad experience during or after you've moved on. That's not your job! Those persons who do such things have to live with themselves so do not mirror that behavior.

Keep Moving Forward

The blessing in disguise here is that you are in charge of your destiny, and your art, as well as making a living with it. Put your energies there. Mirror people who are partaking in good behavior in the arts. Be one of them. Realize that while you're here on this planet, there are differences only you can make.

Keep moving forward and learn new business tools. Avoid collecting dust on your knowledge by applying what you have learned. This is sharing brilliance. Don't just read this book and keep it inside yourself. You do have the power to do anything about your art that you desire. No bulldozing allowed. Speak up without being rude, follow your intuition, apply your talent with love, work it with appreciation, plan it with gratitude, do it and GO! Take Charge of your Big Picture. You are The Boss! You Are The Captain!

So Captain, if you're ready to take charge (which you are or you wouldn't be reading this book), the next piece of the puzzle is creating a business plan, a game plan, to make it a reality.

Perhaps you will choose to open your own art business. So, if you're ready to take charge (which you are or you wouldn't be reading this book), the next piece of the puzzle is creating a business plan, a game plan, to make it a reality. When starting in business you need to decide clearly the blueprint and what it's legal entity should look like. Get a good book on writing a business plan, and actually then write your plan. There are many books on how to write a business plan on amazon.com. One I found very helpful is: Writing a Convincing Business Plan by Arthur R. DeThomas and Lin Grensing-Pophal from Barron's Business Library. Your business plan is not your artist statement or biography. Your business plan needs a clear format and outline. It shows you are serious about your art business and it shows other why they should or should not do business decisions with you in return. This is where you leave your personal feelings and emotions out of the verbiage you are presenting to the world. No one wants to read about your personal problems, challenges or bragging rights here in this document. Be honest in regards to why others should be doing business with you. You need a written business plan in order to do various things in the business world such as incorporate or open a business checking account; as well as a name that is a legal entity. Team up with experts to get your business rolling. Decide what legal identity your business should have. By this I mean, a sole proprietorship, a general ownership, a limited partnership, a C. Corporation, S. Corporation, or an LLC limited liability company.

Don't wait until your art business is up and running to do this. Whether you work out of your home or have a shop, you need to do this legal leg work in setting up your business beforehand. Neglecting this can prove to be a costly mistake. Read up on the differences between the different types of business entities and ask your accountant for the best direction to take. That's right. You'll need professional assistance in areas where you are weak in business, such as an accountant or bookkeeper if you are not good in the numbers area so you can concentrate on creating your art and running business. Learn to delegate your weaknesses for success!

Conduct informational interviews. Interview accountants in your neighborhood to see who works best for your business plan with small business startups. Many professionals, such as accountants and attorneys, offer a free one-time consultation. Some speak at local community business meet-up and networking groups. Take advantage of these services. Interviews require asking questions. Such as: Do you charge by the hour, by the project? How much time does it take you to complete your tasks? What is the best type of business entity for an artist to incorporate under and what are the different types of corporations that exist? How long have you been in business? Have you worked with other artists? What is required of me that I must provide to you for you offer your service the most economically to me? One thing I can guarantee is neat and orderly record keeping in any area of your business will keep cost down from the professional services you hire out.

Find out if you need to be licensed to sell art out of your home. Investigate this thoroughly.

Do you have a friend or relative who is more successful in business than you are? Take them to lunch or coffee and ask them how they started. You'll learn a lot.

Once you've done the legwork, it can be helpful to visualize a symbol of success for your business. What does the symbol of artistic business success look like for you?

Draw a picture of it

We can only see what we are in harmony with. Wealth comes in many forms besides the material. That is external. Having peace of mind may be more important than anything and it may give a feeling of wealth to many people. Good health, loving friends and family are other forms of wealth. Can you think of other forms of wealth that you have already in your life?

Do Your Thoughts Match Your Success Symbol?

Do you have habits or beliefs that are out of sync with your desire to be a successful artist? Example: "In order to become a successful artist, I must sacrifice something or be a ruthless person?"

Do you feel unworthy of being a thriving artist?

Are you angry with some person, organization, or business that treated you poorly?

Do you *really* want to make a living with your art?

These are very important questions to think about and may be deeply embedded into your subconscious crew's day-to-day activities. Answer them and turn them into reverse possibilities as much as possible.

Many folks, including artists, fail in their business for these three reasons:

1. They never decide what they really want to accomplish with their artistry.
2. They don't find out what it takes to get where they want to be with making a living with their art or their business.

3. They fail to get back up when they get down, sidetracked or criticized because they haven't answered questions one and two. They failed to step in and offer creative solutions that utilize their gifts and talents to the so-called people who rejected them .

So identify and decide exactly what you want to accomplish in making a living with your art. Find out what it takes to making a living with your art and keep it running in the direction of YOUR Big Picture. When you run into obstacles keep moving forward and focus on what you really want to accomplish. You may find out that you have many other talents that your art amplifies such as a love for coordinating projects or writing, a teacher, negotiator and that being an artist is just a feather in your cap that others require your services for. Remember as mentioned earlier you can find greater business success by finding ways to be of service and enrich lives by solving other people's problems with your talent.

Chapter Three's Studio Play Sheet

Write a memo to your subconscious crew.

In the memo thank them for doing a great job and give them an uplifting pep talk in the mirror. Tell them what you are going to accomplish today.

At the end of the day thank them for their assistance and ask them an empowering question, something like, "What happened to cause success to come to me?" (Your subconscious mind is like a million super computers and will go to work to answer the questions while you sleep… your crew never sleeps.)

Upon waking, record any new dream insights. Many of the world's greatest discoveries and inspirations came through dreams.

Ask yourself if there are any areas where you can grow and focus on developing those areas.

When crisis should arrive, pause, breathe and step back. Before reacting to your ego with fear, ask, "What would the captain and crew do?"

Take time when making decisions and allow yourself the opportunity to check in with your higher source through meditation or prayer

How much are you living in accord with your deepest truest artist self? Let things happen when you get in touch with your true inner artist self.

How much positive influence do your talents have on the world? Did you know you could impact more people with your talent than you realize at any given moment in a positive and powerful way?

As an artist, how much co-creating do you do with others? It's easier to create amazing things with others when you let go of the control, releasing the need to dominate.

There is no reason for you to suffer or struggle your way to or through anything, be it your art career or any career. Choose your Big Picture of life, give your attention to it and find the good feeling place of being there. Meditate, reflect upon it and appreciate the Big Picture of your dreams as if it's already there and be there with it in your heart and mind. Suit up, show up and be of service to different venues with your divine talents. Tell people about what you are doing and then listen for the nudges from the Universe, from folks around you, the places you visit, the music you hear, all the sights, sounds, feelings that are showing up to guide you to your Big Picture. Make it bigger and go for the biggest picture in your mind and heart with love.

Draw a symbol of what artist success looks like to you. Something simple that represents you thriving, prosperous and loving life as the artist you are. Is there more than one symbol? Draw them all.

Creative Activity Points

First and foremost, as in any business including the artist business, you must have a business plan in place and follow that format.

Be open to adjust your business plan as your art career grows.

Don't assume that anyone who reads it will know your artistic jargon. A business plan is not an artist biography or statement. It explains in simple terms how you will be making income and why people will want to do business with you. When you write your business plan it should be easy to read, realistic and understandable.

Decide on what it is your legal business entity is based on your business plan. Keep your personal life out of your business plan.

Your art business plan always conveys the large and profitable market opportunities for the business, as well as your strength in carrying out its ongoing growth.

Take up local business offers on free consultations such as accountants and attorneys by conducting informational interviews.

Attend local business chamber meetings and business mixers as a guest to see what is going on in the community. Are any other artisans attending? If not, you may be a big fish in a small pond. This is an opportunity to share your gifts!

See if your city or town offers classes and seminars to local businesses. These are usually free and offered through the tax and business licensing offices.

Find out if you need to have a business license to sell art out of your home.

You win in business when you refused to be discouraged by defeat.

Always be gracious and professional and operate from the outcome, even if you just started, you can be in the mindset of success. In other words, to avoid the: I just started, apologetic syndrome. When you keep telling the stories of how you're not as good or talented or how you got ripped off then you are accepting the role of victim. The people that you do business with will mirror that. Unless you want those types of business associates and partners, take those degrading old stories out of your Big Picture right away! Tell people, "I am the artist, photographer, writer, musician etc. and I operate a very successful business."

Studios should look like a place of work and galleries should look clean and professional.

Celebrate other folks' wins just as though they are yours. Go team!

A business card is the single most requested item you will be asked for.

You must have a business card that includes a sample of your art and your contact information. Be sure that your business card is two sided. A one sided business card is twice as likely to be overlooked and thrown away.

Every single bit of art and information about your art must include your contact information.

Your business card, logo, business forms, website, correspondence and social media presence must be truthful symbols of your artistic business success. This is vital since it represents your new story and will be powerfully conveyed to the world.

Wealth comes in many forms, not just money. Bartering and trading are good examples of wealth exchanges in business. Give unconditional value to all, including other artists.

Your business patterns should be in sync with your values and habits. You may have to change habits and beliefs in order to create thriving business patterns.

Never question your talent. Work on your inner drive, which helps your talent shine and directs it where it needs to go. Know what you want and always bring it on! Make it fun and play Show and Tell with Passion!

CHAPTER FOUR

Share What You Love to Do – Telling is Selling

"Be who you are and say what you feel, because those who mind don't matter and those who matter don't mind." —Dr. Seuss

CHASING HAPPY

Many single people spend countless hours on the Internet, singles bars and coffee shops flaunting themselves. They are trying to land the perfect partner, boyfriend, girlfriend, date or fun rendezvous. What are they doing? They are marketing themselves with some sort of sales presentation. They meet THE ONE and yet continue to be miserable and disappointed. Do they give up? Usually not. They keep persisting until the Big Picture of their partner is met.

Other folks do this very same thing with work. They market themselves on paper and go on interviews to get better pay at the dream job or, just any old job for that matter. If these amazing marketers are "lucky," they get hired, get the dream job and the same thing happens like the dating pool mentioned above. Off they go to the so-called dream job and before long they are miserable, unsatisfied, disgruntled, laid off and promoted up and out. Do they give up? Perhaps, but most often they market to a new employer, sell themselves into a new job and on it goes.

Some folks play keeping up with the Joneses with the perfect house, cars, clothes, lifestyle, looking good on the outside while feeling miserable on the inside. Do they stop doing it? No, they keep going. Shall I continue with more examples of people searching on the outside for things to fill up what they are missing on the inside?

WHAT ARE YOU MARKETING?

What are they doing? You could call this chasing "Happy" but happy never comes. They are marketing to the wrong people but marketing, nonetheless. So many people do this it has become natural. Marketing is not advertising, PR or selling; marketing is a process of the ongoing story of you, and what you do, that story you are telling others! Advertising is the activity of numbers going out, money and expecting money to come in. You'd better know what you're doing. PR is telling people through media what you are marketing. Here again you get what you pay for. Selling is the action of numbers coming in, money from the effects of marketing. We have been doing it since the caveman days. Based on your old beliefs, you could market yourself to everything that is less than what you really want and need for your unique journey. You could wind up in the same old place where you started wondering how the heck that happened. What are you marketing and to whom are you marketing? You are marketing YOU. Market wherever you desire!

If you are unhappy with the results of your art sales, you must stop doing what you're doing.

Open Your Heart and Take a Good Look Inside

There is good news and it comes with a change in behavior. You must begin with an inside sales job on yourself first. In other words your first sale is to yourself. It is very important to love what you are doing from your heart. I am not talking about feeling self-important. I am talking about opening up your heart. Are you sold on your own services before someone else pays you money?

Open up your eyes and ears to what lies just beneath the surface in your heart, your inner wealth. Enough is enough already!!

Are there things you keep doing that get in the way in your art career or daily activities, even habits that you do not want to repeat but do? Write those things down. What you want is usually the opposites of those things!

Did you do this? If not, what are you waiting for? Another dead end result? Procrastination is the biggest artist time waster and career killer out there.

Write them down. The faster you turn your attention to your solutions and away from what doesn't work, the better. Continuing to dwell on the things you don't want just attracts more of the same.

Once you have your 'unwanted things' list, what are the opposites? Do you want those things that are opposite of the things you do not want? If so, write them down on two separate pieces of paper. Now you have a sheet of what you want and one of what you don't want. Toss the sheet with ones that you are not interested in. Make a ritual and tear that list up, burn it if you can or shred it! Do not revisit things you don't want. It is time to move on.

The inside sales job on yourself is where The Big Picture Roadmap begins. Start the process and you're on the way to discover yourself first.

It's All About the Journey

Personal success is not a finished product, end result, fame or gold pot at the end of the rainbow. Success is personal and all about the journey. It is about enjoying and loving every bit of it, the dreaming of it and the unfolding of your life. Success is the happy journey from here to there.

For me, the fun in making art is in dreaming it up, making it and sharing a story about how it all came about, some of my paintings depict historically significant places or themes. I learn about the subject, it inspires me. I may even put myself or friends into the picture, then share the story about it. It creates interest and that is what sells it. Good old-fashioned Show and Tell. When I'm done with my painting, my journey continues onward. The inside sales job you are doing is the opening up and sharing of your inner creative wealth. Artists as creators have a wealth that must be shared with the world. These gifts are inside you and don't cost you anything. Your inner wealth is your responsibility to be shared with others so they can thrive. Only you can do it. Only you know how to market it best. Only you can sell yourself in the best ways. What does inner wealth mean to you? Knowing this is what creates your life's Big Picture.

If there is only one thing you get out of reading this book about the business of art, let it be this-The person who is better at telling their art's story will outsell the person who has a better product EVERYTIME. Your art is a product and so is the story that you share along with it. Just go to a museum or gallery space and stand in front of an abstract and wait to hear other person's critical comments. Here's one I love. The brutal and fear based cliché, "I could have painted that with my feet." Well, one has to ask, "If you are an artist, why didn't you?" What do you imagine the artist who made the painting said when it was presented for sale? They most likely made a courageous presentation about themselves and their abstract work, selling their exciting ideas to a collector, client, or directly to the museum. Through the artist's impeccable and sincere marketing and enthusiastic story, a re-occurring value and worth in investment dollars has now been recognized. And it sells! It was just too delicious to resist! You don't need to be good at selling; that's hard work. What you need is a good marketing presentation, which is more than a pretty portfolio or slick website.

A Winning Attitude Wins

You always share your talented inner wealth with the world through your attitudes, which can be controlled. Conversely, you have no control over outside circumstances, like weather or other people. It's good to remember this. You do have some control with moods, feelings and emotions that come and go. This determines how you express feelings through your attitude. Your internal attitude makes or breaks your external marketing experience. It's where your value begins to shine and take form.

People often say to me that I am always so nice or always so happy. They always want to know how I do it. Do I always feel this way? No, but I continually choose an attitude of gratitude and before long I am pretty happy. There are some fun gratitude exercises to try as you move through this book. I'm sure you will enjoy doing them over and over again and sharing them with others. Good attitudes are contagious.

It's All About Show and Tell!

As I mentioned in the beginning of this book, besides being an artist, I'm a marketer as well. How did I learn marketing? I learned it in kindergarten a long time ago. It was the game of "show and tell" and it had to do with the things I love. That is what I do today and that's what I want to do throughout the remainder of my life. When an artist sees something in their mind and creates something else with a picture, a song, writing, and so on it is a story that inspires others. Guess what? That's what we all do as well, whether you know it or not, or love it or not. We are all playing the game of show and tell for others and ourselves while painting our Big Picture.

The way to win in business is to market with integrity and grace and by telling a true story. You must believe the story you are telling or the public won't. Then, you'll be happy and satisfied with what you are marketing. You are naturally attracted to what you are marketing, which is your art! When you love and are attracted to what you are marketing, people are attracted to you. You become a magnet for a successful Big Picture. That's the technique; it's your magnetism. What a great way to be rewarded!

What's *Your* Magnetic Story?

When you are a magnet for your ideal Big Picture instead of chasing people and situations, they are attracted to you naturally.

So what's your magnetic story? The one you're attached to on the inside? The one instilled in you growing up, the art story you heard others speak of? Many artists hang on to their suffering stories like badges of courage. They do this in order to protect themselves instead of letting go of the fear and suffering. They end up pushing away the very thing they want and magnetize the very thing they don't want. Sounds crazy when you stand back and look at how we all do this, yet, it's so common with everyone, not just artists. What story are you telling to yourself and others? Whether it's good or bad, can you let go of your story? Could you drop it? Could you just be?

If playing the struggling artist no longer serves you then you must drop that false persona, divorce it, move on and start being your authentic self. Isn't that a relief? Lighten your load and burdening thoughts by letting go of that starving artist story. It's only a story, probably someone else's, told to you many different times in different ways. It's not who you are, so stop acting like it is. When I told people I lost my job they bombarded with their sad stories right back. No wonder everyone including myself felt awful. So I changed my story, I dropped the laid off story completely. I began telling a new story which was that I was pursuing my art career full time. Guess what? That new story changed everything for the positive and new art sales opportunities began to appear quickly. People like stories of success and they attract the right people, circumstances and sales opportunities. Make a declaration to yourself right now to drop old stories that do not serve your Big Picture.

Marketing is Like Kissing

Marketing your story is sort of like kissing - if you like what you're marketing, you lean into it. If you're sincere about it, your prospect, situation or success story will lean into you. In order to get that first kiss, you have to spend a little time and develop a relationship with what you really want. You have to be sure you want that first kiss, because where it leads is into a new relationship. Be sure you want it – or not.

One of the greatest bits of advice that an independent artist business owner can get is this- you must know yourself first and then your customer. It is not about your product. That's advertising. When you advertise, you'd better know what you're doing or you'll be flushing lots of money down the drain. It's about marketing and that's people, relationships, collaboration and rapport. You do this by connecting with stories that bring you both joy and love. This is what it is ALL about.

Create more time for people, time for yourself and space to relate to others and you will expand your own joy in the process. Chase sales, money, bank statements and you will be worn out; your money, business, customers and clients will leave as soon as you engage them.

What is your story and what is their story and how can you connect the two? To do this you must know yourself, who your customer is and how you can make each other's lives better. Sharing, creating harmony and building trust are part of success. That is marketing at its finest.

Drop your old stories of lack, be courageous and confident, and think about what you actually want to share. Open your mouth and speak about what you love to do just like when you are in love! That's marketing and that's what will sell you and your art product. That is what will make other people sell your product without you even knowing it. You'll know that's happening when your product goes viral. It begins with you.

Today "Going Viral" is an important option for marketing your art. Using social networks to market your art to others with, pictures, messages, newsletters and videos to people who intern share through their large networks you can tap into a big customer base like never before. However without incentives to spread the message this approach can fizzle as quickly as it snowballed. This is where research and talking to experts in the field saves lots of time.

Creative Activity Points

Here's something to think about. Like kissing, most people who say they are good at selling are not. With 'marketing your story' practice, you can naturally become better without even realizing it.

Speak about what you love from the heart and your art will sell itself.

Plan ahead where you will sell and distribute your art.

Decide what type of e-mail and web marketing you will use.

Decide if you will advertise and be sure to know your target audience and how often you plan to advertise.

Decide if you will have others involved in the sales and representation of your art. If there are other people doing this how will they be compensated?

What type of P.R. (public relations) will you use?

What type of efficient direct marketing (postcards, flyers, business cards) will you use? Do you plan to create these yourself or outsource them?

How will people recognize you and your art product? Brand all of your marketing materials cohesively to establish identity.

Keep an eye out for recent trends then apply your art skills to those trends.

You are your number one promoter! Always carry your professionally printed, double sided business cards. Create personalized stationery and a website to match. Brand yourself; tell your story, then let it go.

Ask for referrals.

Create a written plan for achieving your marketing and publicity goals.

In order to achieve your goals, seek guidance from a marketing expert to ensure your strategy is sound.

A marketing plan must have a good balance between being comprehensive and realistic. It can be very simple.

Being a great artist has little or no value if no one knows about your fabulous talent and craft.

When people who can and want to help realize that you know what you want and what you are talking about, doors will open for you.

M.B. Rollercoaster

STUDIO TWO

A Magical Mind

Don't believe everything You Think.

Train Yourself with Clarity.

Step Two: Beliefs Influence Genius.

CHAPTER FIVE

Thinking your Big Picture Correctly

*"What we are is God's gift to us.
What we become is our gift to God."*
—Eleanor Powell

I grew up in Connecticut in a wealthy suburb of New York City. Many of the locals created their living by working long, hard hours. My family was not one of these well-to-do old money families; however we did know many of them, as my relatives worked with and for them in different capacities. Most were lovely people. Some were tycoons and captains of industry. Their wealth brought their families lavish lifestyles while others chose less opulence, yet they still lived very well indeed. Some made and lost great fortunes and created them all over again; some had regular jobs, some volunteered at their favorite charities and some just played and had fun. Many spent time vacationing all over the world enjoying free time with family and friends. Fun time didn't have to be a choice; with no financial struggle, these people lived well. Long after the breadwinner died at an early age , these families continued to live well with their new spouses and partners and children enjoying the hard-working legacy left behind.

Two Types of Wealthy, Two Different Mindsets

There were two notable types of wealthy groups.
One type of these folks would get up at four in the morning to take the train into the city, working until eight o'clock in the evening. They then returned, taking the commuter train back to their homes and to their families in those bucolic and swanky suburbs.
The other type of wealthy folks generated income with half the effort in half the time and enjoyed their families all the time. They lived to a ripe old age and enjoyed their creations. Like those other wealthy families, they too, accumulated and lost wealth and regained it again.
It appeared with both types of families that the more they wealth they had, the more they gave away and the more they created. Occasionally, you would hear the tragic dramatic story of the silver spooned one who lost it all but they were the exception to the rule and continue to be

so. The cycles appeared to indicate that the rich got richer, but there was a distinct difference between the two old money types.

The contrast between the two types of wealth-building families was the way in which they created their wealth, the quality of life they chose to live and how they utilized their time. Both mindsets were brilliant; the only difference was one worked smarter and the other worked harder. Through asking empowering questions, one tycoon had a better system for creating wealth in his earning environment. This benefited longevity and his beliefs were passed down to the next generation in the family.

Now, going to the opposite extreme of not working won't cut it, either. Life requires balance. An artist's living takes value-producing work in order to create the life you want. How you believe you can create that work to produce your fortune is the difference between being healthy and happy and literally drop-dead filthy rich. In a strange contradiction of life, you could actually be very wealthy financially and still be a starving artist emotionally.

Artists-In-Residence

In the area where I lived, there were also many well-known artists and writers and some were extremely wealthy. Popular suburban towns in that area have easy access to the nearby New York City via highways or the railroad. Just up the road from our house was the large estate, Stormfield, where Mark Twain lived out his last years. Twain even founded our town's public library in Redding Connecticut.

Because of the somewhat close proximity to New York, on clear days the Empire State Building, the Chrysler Building and the twin towers of the World Trade Center could be seen from some of the hilltops. To a child it was a magical place just out of reach. I was fascinated with the city and the great public pieces of art there. Going to the big city was always very exciting. Most of all I was enthralled with the Statue of Liberty, which I constantly drew, as well as the Empire State or Chrysler building. At this particular time in my life I couldn't get away from the subject of buildings in my drawing my pictures. Even today I have one of my Empire State building pictures in my home; architecture runs heavily in most of my art themes.

Mrs. Huntington

In my childhood it was not uncommon for some of these artistic residents to be guests, speaking to students at school. In first grade a visitor spoke to our art class. I loved art class and was always excited when a guest visited and spoke about what they did, especially artists. This guest was a sweet little old lady, a local resident and an artist. Her name was Mrs. Huntington. It seemed everyone in town knew her because of the bronze statues she made. One of her beautiful statues was on the front lawn of our school.

On the day Mrs. Huntington came to our art class, she spoke to us about being an artist. I remember her asking who wanted to also be an artist when they grew up. I think at the time most of the hands in the class went up and then she'd walk around the room as we made our little doodles. When she came over to me and said hello I asked her, "Did you make the statue in front of our school?" "Yes, I did," she answered. Then I asked. "Did you make the Statue of Liberty in New York too?" She laughed and told me that another artist had made that. "Well that's good because it's not as pretty as the statue in front of our school." She laughed again, patted me on the head. and said, "It is a very beautiful statue, isn't it? It's a very special and important piece of art." I never forgot those words. She instilled in me the early belief that art was important.

The Thrift Shop Ladies

In most of these beautiful towns there were thrift shops run by local charities. Not all, but some of the ladies who volunteered at the shops were from those wealthy and powerful families. My grandmother would take me there to find art books. Nonie, as I called her, would say, "This is my grandson; he's an artist." We talked a little about art and if we were fortunate, the shop might have had an art book to purchase for a dime or a quarter. Or if it was really special it might be a whole dollar! A huge sum of money for me! When I got home I would devour the information, ask questions about the artists in the book and copy the pictures inside.

I remember the thrift shop ladies would talk about how they could make things in the world better and more beautiful with art. Sometimes they would host charity event parties to help people all around the world and at the same time discuss a piece of art by a famous artist or a new local artist they discovered. They sometimes invited these artists, ranging from actors, singers to painters to lend their talent to their causes. When the ladies talked about money, I'd hear some interesting things that were different than what I heard other people talking about. When the subject of not enough money would come up they would say things like, "Oh, I would never think that way," or "What good things for the community are you going to do your new investment return?" I'd hear things about their amazing big plans, and then later read about the very thing they discussed in the paper or see it on the news! They'd ask me what I was going to be or do when I grew up. I'd say, "I'm going to be an artist!" They'd tell me that was brilliant and that the world needed more artists than ever. Never a peep of struggle was ever mentioned. It was very interesting to me how they seemed to understand how I felt about being an artist.

House-Sitting

As an older responsible teenager I was asked to house sit for some of the better off folks I had met and befriended over the years. I was a little house-sitting business entrepreneur and for a week or two during my stays, I was surrounded by the finer things in life, including famous paintings and priceless antiques. I acted as if I was already enjoying the benefits of my illustrious art career in my own home. But deep down something told me I was less than this. They were different from me, this was make-believe, and I wasn't one of them.

My close and extended family continued to reinforce this idea of being different and talked about the rich and famous artists who were making fortunes. In the same breath, they'd say "You can't do that. You're not one of them. We're different. Become a minister or a missionary. Do something useful."

On My Own

Why? I thought. I was an artist and this didn't make any sense. Why did they get me so interested in art in the first place? I began to rebel and join in the blame game. I began to struggle with my identity, my sexuality and with who I was as a man. I had to get out of there. I had to be an artist, it was in my blood and God made me that way. I was determined to do it on my own but those seeds of doubt were already planted. My blame game had started- it was everyone else's fault why I couldn't do what I loved.

I got sidetracked in my thinking as a young adult venturing into the world on my own. Influenced by well-meaning persons who I loved and who didn't know any better, I bought into their starving artist mentality.

I got away and moved to California, where I had relatives in the Los Angeles area. I loved being there; it was so very different. I thought the California relatives would be more open minded. Not so! I got into relationships with people who also had the same beliefs about artists, or even worse ones! Gradually I realized if anyone was going to help me believe I could be an artist it had to be me, first and foremost. Otherwise, I'd just keep getting the same story over and over again with the same lousy ending.

Time for a Change, Or Two Or Three

Broke and tired, I decided to take full responsibility for my life. I picked myself up and changed my thinking. The belief that I indeed could be a thriving and prosperous artist which I had from a young age, was still in there somewhere. I remembered some of those wealthy folks back in Connecticut who had said that they had gone broke more than once, making and losing fortunes. But they were never "poor." There was a difference in being broke and being poor!

I needed to learn about money so I got a job as a banker, where I soon learned that unless you owned the place, all the money in banking was in the vault.

Next, I had a career in Human Resources, where I learned some valuable people skills. This is where I truly realized that many people just like me where not doing what they loved. When they offered me promotions, something inside always told me *NO. You can paint; you're a painter.* I have learned that it's okay to say no and sometimes it's absolutely necessary.

Deciding not to look back, I asked myself lots of questions about what I really wanted. I moved quite a few times back and forth from coast to coast searching for the answers. I worked for my family in their Connecticut retail business before going back to California and eventually landed in beautiful San Diego. The interesting thing was that every time I did something with my art I thrived and every time I ignored it, I didn't do so well.

Synchronicity in San Diego

Everyone seems to be in love with San Diego. *There's good energy there*, I thought. I was being offered art shows there, so I went for it. That little internal voice told me, *YES!* I remembered hearing about beautiful Balboa Park and the Marston family, whose legacy included the creation of the great city park and its fabulous golden age architecture here in California.

Enormous Balboa Park would be such a lovely place to paint. I'd often see artists working outdoors. After my move I ventured over to the park to explore. One particular park visit was different. I asked myself, *What is it that am I supposed to be doing here? How could I share my gifts with the world?*

Walking around amongst the incredible Spanish colonial buildings, I saw the centerpiece of the central Plaza Panama which was a huge bronze statue. I didn't recall ever seeing it before yet it seemed strangely familiar. It had a noble warrior carrying a flag while riding a horse. I walked over to it and read the inscription, feeling it was an obvious sign.

"Oh my goodness! Of course!" I gasped aloud.

It read: "El Cid by Anna Hyatt Huntington."

WOW! Mrs. Huntington made this sculpture! The lady from the art class who told me art was important! Suddenly everything was clear, I made a decision right then and there to be a warrior in thinking the right way about my art and being around people who also thought positively about art and wealth. I conquered and decided to slay that poor-starving-artist-mentality dragon with El Cid as my witness. There was hope! Some people call this a miracle while others might call it a moment of clarity. I've had many, many of them. The more I have them, the more empowering questions I ask of myself.

Ask Empowering Questions

Hoping is good but making a decision is better. To move in the direction of good decisions from now on ask empowering questions of yourself. Here is a good question to start you off with- What could I do that doubles my art income and productivity?

Instead of hoping for the art show, *decide* what it will look like, where it will be and what the degree of its success will be. For example, "I am thoroughly enjoying the outrageous success of my sold out art show!"

You cannot have an answer without being able to ask the question. If you can think up the question there is an answer to it. It need not be answered right away. Ask the question and be sure it is empowering. The answer will come. It must. Decide your outcome will be success from this point forward.

No more effort is required to aim for a fabulously successful artist career than is required to accept misery and poverty. All things are possible. Being a starving artist is not required to have a thriving artist's career. Begin to shatter those old myths now and ask empowering questions to reverse limiting thinking. Slay that dragon of a story.

What are you Feeding your Mind?

Even though it may appear sometimes that success only comes to certain people, the process of success is not random or haphazard. You have a magical mind akin to a super computer and will process anything you feed into it. That's its job. Success follows thought and thought follows energy. Energy is the pure vibration or spirit of which we are all made. Sometimes the thoughts that you feed your mind might not be all that good for you. Garbage in – garbage out. Negative things and thoughts such as, *I can't seem to do anything right* or *I'll never be this or that*, is like feeding your brain junk food. Don't believe everything you think and question what you are feeding your mind.

You train your mind by deciding what you will feed it and how you utilize your time. What you create begins with a thought. The way you think and what comes from it, successful or not, is its manifestation. You create clear agreements first with yourself through your thinking. You must speak of abundance freely and often, remembering past successes as positive evidence and failures as new opportunities to grow. Our thoughts and feelings literally become things, no matter how small - they have power!

As you focus on the things you love and visualize the future that you want, relax into it and remember what you want afterwards. By doing this you are choosing to give yourself the best life ever, right now, in the here and now. Your ability to do this is unlimited. Your ability to thrive and prosper is natural because that is who you are. As you apply creative wisdom to daily action, surrounding yourself with loving supporting relationships you will be nourished. Your development will be guided in ways that honor your essence. You will be brought closer to your Soul's higher purpose. By remembering and seeing the future you want, you're naturally magnetized to persons that strengthen, inspire and empower you to become all that you are capable of being. You become more aware and see things with a new appreciation, through joy, as you apply your wisdom and share your joy and thanks. You learn how to create support and walk your own path as you provide value and service in all you do. Your artist spirit is the ultimate creator and wants you to be successful.

You don't gain or lose a lot of excess weight overnight from starting or stopping to eat things that aren't good for you; it takes a plan followed through with work. The same goes for what you feed you mind. It takes persistence, exercise, work and dedication. The good news is the road to becoming successful is a basic and simple diet. You deliberately choose good thoughts, beliefs and ideas from the desirable outcome you wish to manifest.

You can now be aware that what is showing up in your life is a direct outcome of how you used your creativity in the past. The way you have used your mind translates into the life you have today.

One of the best ways to conquer frustration and anxiety, while making a living as an artist is a willingness to learn a new truth. Start to do this right now by dropping habitual and untrue and useless ideas. Stop blaming the world and others for not being able to make a living with your art. How about starting with dropkicking the starving artist fantasy? If you have an idea about the way things are ask yourself is it true. Is it true that all artists are starving? Are you starving? If it's not true, drop it and don't waste your energy there ever again. Living based on the unfounded is a waste of life.

Value truth above everything; it's okay to be wrong if necessary. Don't let anything, including false ideas, block your search to make a living as an artist. Frustration is often caused by useless and false ideas, which create anxiety. Have the willingness to give up all the old ideas and learn new truthful ones.

Here's a quick review:

Train your mind by what you feed it through your diet of thoughts.
Ask yourself empowering questions; slay lots of mythical dragons.
You're either on a good or a bad diet. You know what diet you're on by the ensuing results in your life, your career and your relationships. These are all good indicators.
You can change your art business results by being aware of your thoughts and by being willing to think healthier ones. This will change your mental and emotional diet.
Take care of your mind and body, and they take care of you.
Change hoping into decisive-outcome thinking by picturing and declaring what you want to link with your artist creative spirit.

Chapter Five's Studio Play Sheet

Thinking in bigger, expanded and healthier ways creates a clear Big Picture.

The objective of this play sheet is to creatively stretch what you want into something bigger, broader and have fun with brainstorming on your own. From your prior lists of what you can do, write down all the ways you can take these things and stretch them bigger than you first imagined.

Your life is your blank canvas. What would you intentionally create for yourself? It's okay to be selfish here, this is playtime; allow yourself to dream and Go Big! Turn off the T.V. and close the newspaper. The sky is the limit, so reach!

Take all the paper you need, in fact, I would get a blank spiral notebook and be quiet for a few minutes while thinking about all the possibilities. Begin writing, dreaming and writing more. For example if you want to have an art show, where specifically do you want to have the art show? What city or town, in what sort of a venue? How many pieces of art? Is a solo or group show? Draw a floor plan of the show, draw what the outside of the building where your art is looks like, How about sketching a picture of a billboard announcing your art show, stretch it, make it bigger. Write about the opening event, who is attending and what sort of refreshments, music, entertainment, and what will you dress like? Keep it going till there is nothing left to think of. Write them out and then simplify it and draw a stick figure of what it represents on a sticky note. Look at your image in quiet; reflect on the good feelings it caused you to feel inside. Do this for all the exercises in this chapter.

What productive things can you create? Write them down and draw a stick figure of it/them on a sticky note.

1. What are some small successes you have had this week?
2. Can you create more small successes this week? What would they be? Draw a stick figure of them on a sticky note.
3. Would you create more income for yourself and others? Your family?

Draw a simple stick figure of it on a sticky note.

4. What are the many benefits derived from your creations in unexpected and marvelous ways? Write it out, then literally draw the line, a stick figure of it on a sticky note, post it where you see it often and meditate on the image. Look at your image in quiet; reflect on the good feelings it caused you to feel inside. This can be a vital piece of the Big Picture!
5. Would you travel or stay home more?
6. Where does your success bring you?

Draw a stick figure of it on a sticky note.

7. What is your million-dollar idea?

Draw a stick figure of it on a sticky note.

8. What other ideas can you come up with?
9. What objectives could you practice today and this week which will assist you in focusing in order to achieve you goals?
10. Now, ask yourself this. What one desire can I give my full attention to for one week? Decide to do it.

Use these next questions to assist in the things you want to focus upon.

11. Are you working towards one thing and expecting another? Make sure you are working towards a career you really love or else what you want in your art career will not happen. When you are expecting big things to happen in your life, then you really have to prepare mentally for them first, laying the ground work for those things you love to happen.
12. What are you doing today and what good are you expecting to happen? Are they a match?
13. How do you spend your time?

Stop and think about whether you are mastering how you want to make a living with what you want to be as an artist now?

If not, do you know that if you take two hours a day, seven days a week to study anything about it equals about two years worth of full-time, 40-hour work weeks? Think about that. You can learn a lot about anything!

14. Where are you going to be in five years with making a living your art? Will you be working on what you want to create with your art career or will you still be putting off what you want to do?

Creative Activity Points

People will ask you when and why you became an artist and why you decided to form and found an art company. Keep your philosophy short, honest and to the point on this. One line answers are best. You will lose them after about three or four. Lose them in conversation and you lose the sale.

When you feel love for your art career, people will feel that love too and simply have to have your art.

The story or hidden belief you hang onto is what others believe. They can feel this just by being around your energy. Let go of stories that created the victimized-starving-artist-romance from the past and which held you back.

Believe you are worthy of being a successful and thriving artist and expect others to see you in that same light.

Always clearly introduce yourself, your art company and your business. For example, "Hi! My name is RD; I'm the artist and these are all of my paintings. Welcome to my studio and gallery."

Everyone loves success. Be prepared to answer when others ask why they should invest in your art.

Move forward with love every day treasuring your thriving artist Big Picture. Add value to the world by being your authentic artist self.

Be willing to give up all the old ideas and to learn new truthful ways of being.

Focus. Invest two hours a day, seven days a week studying the information that you want to master. In five years you'll have mastered quite a lot of knowledge.

Utilize your time well, focusing five full minutes per day on the thing you really want to be doing.

CHAPTER SIX

Be Aware of Your Fears and Turning Them Around

"The cave you fear to enter holds the treasure you seek." —Joseph Campbell

I had some amazing teachers back in my high school like Joel Barlow in Redding, Connecticut. I can't begin to express my gratitude for the time they took to help shape and encourage my confused young mind. As a result, they instilled in me a sense of exploration that has taken me all the way to becoming a professional artist as well as a best-selling author. Amazing!

One teacher in particular, Mrs. Cubeta, had a special English, Art and Photography project we all worked on. She scheduled a field trip to The British Art Collection at Yale in New Haven where she showed us an exhibit of a new painter, David Hockney. When I saw his paintings and drawings, I innately sensed that I too could become a successful painter. How so? Because those paintings and drawings were what I wanted to make but was afraid to, scenes stuck in my head, and there they were hanging in front of me in a prestigious place and they were accepted.

As I looked at those paintings hanging in a world-class museum, the fear and angst I had carried as a developing young man, from my sexual orientation to what was to become of me suddenly disappeared; I felt better about myself as a person. All was well and felt I belonged in the world. Art is that powerful.

I had an amazing realization about that day many years later. In 1997 when I was doing a book signing about my paintings in that very same building at Yale, I met one of my favorite artists. Paul Cadmus, America's greatest living figurative artist at the time and I spent an entire hour talking under a beautiful oak tree at a University party being thrown in his honor. It seemed that no one was interested as I was in hearing his about art and artist's fears. I had just received a bad review and I was aware that he had also had his share of bad reviews over the years. I'll never forget what he said to me that day. "First of all, you hit a nerve in that critic which means you're doing something right. Don't let a silly thing like fear stop you from your brilliance; keep leaving them clues about what a real artist you truly are."

Those were magical days. I must humbly thank my teachers and mentors who guided and lit the path to my passions. Because of these talented and wisdom-filled people, my experiences continue to blossom today as an artist and writer.

THE F WORD

There are clues to getting on the road to success where your Big Picture awaits. One of the biggest clues is The F word.

The thing that stops us is FEAR. The fear list goes on forever for most artists. It usually begins with a "yeah, but" statement or excuse. Here are some common fears.

Fear of : pressure, making poor decisions and looking foolish, not being smart enough, not knowing what to do, the unknown, being alone, being smothered, changing our habits, and fear of change. Everybody screams, "We want change!" However, what most people are saying is, "We don't want to personally change…we want *you to change for us* and make us all better." Fear isn't real unless it's life threatening.

Basically Fear is this: F.E.A.R. False Evidence Appearing Real.

Fear is an instinctual survival skill, which we have muscled up to justify our excuses for having No Clear Vision of what we want. The truth is that fear is a thin wall standing right in front of the thing you want. What are your fears regarding making a living as an artist? What are your fears about simply living as an artist?

When you receive rejection you are no worse off than before the rejection. You're still in the same place. Not a lesser place.

Your artist spirit is always happy to reveal your truth if you are willing to hear it. Your ego is always willing to hide your truth and keep you stuck, blocked and safe by going in circles. When we accept fear, we create more doubt and inconsistency, which we analyze, intellectualize and justify, feeding more fear to others and ourselves. We continue to feed our over hungry ego factory.

Many folks waste precious time going into battle to destroy the ego. You can't; it's a natural part of you. Besides, your artist spirit loves every bit of you including your ego. It merely looks upon the ego as an over active chattering kid in the classroom. You don't have to surrender to your ego; instead, surrender to your inner artist spirit and your soul which desires you to have love and longs for your artistic success and happiness.

FEAR OF REJECTION

Did you know that fear of rejection is the single greatest reason artists do not make money in art sales? Fear of rejection is a big blocker for most folks. By actually going out and inviting rejection, you overcome your fear in stages; here's what happens:

Stage 1. You get rejected and it bothers you, *like an annoying friend.*

Stage 2. You get rejected and it doesn't bother you. *Well you're my friend, so I forgive you.*

Stage 3. You get rejected and turn it to your advantage. *Yes, yes, I get you; let's work with this.*

Stage 4. You get it and you have fun with it. *OKAY! Let's roll up our sleeves and make something good happen here.*

Here's something else and it's BIG. Action Cures Fear. A fear-based ego quiets down when work appears; the last thing the ego wants to do is work, which ruins its regal importance. The ego sends its friend fear to do its dirty work, keeping itself safe and comfortable. So you can blame fear for all the things you don't accomplish. Oh, that lazy friend of fear! Yes, they are friends. They are trying to protect themselves and you too, by playing it safe.

Can you hear them squawking? They will both eventually quiet down as you work. Why? Because, the ego is LAZY and it is coaching fear with no integrity. You've got to separate those two best friends. The fearful ego will either quit, walk off the job or you may have to fire it. In business, the sooner you get rid of the disruptive employee, the better. You're in the business of joy, remember? Take a deep breath and send fear and ego love, thank them for trying to protect you, and then mentally send them on separate vacations. They deserve a rest.

Fear Vs. Anger

If you weren't afraid of doing a certain thing, what is it that you would do?
You must get into action to do it or else fear is going to pester and nag you until you rise to the occasion and calm it down. Fear wants you to say it's OKAY to be scared so that it can relax, especially if it's had a rough workout and its muscle is ready to snap. Your ego wants you to react differently, most often with anger. It feels that at any given time there's an over abundance of angry artists out there. If you're an angry artist, you may get attention but eventually it will take a toll on your art business. Anger alerts everyone to avoid doing business with certain persons. Seek professional help if your anger is controlling your art.

Fear vs. Your Inner Artist Spirit

Fear will also alert your inner artist spirit, which is your innate directive, to a sort of GPS system saying, "Investigate something else; something better is here in this situation". It sends a gentle nudge encouraging you to pay attention. "Don't go there; here is an opportunity lurking over this way or that way…go here." Get it? However, if you ignore your inner artist long enough you will silence it. Instead of being drowned and addicted to fear, which the world loves, put it to work and use it to tap into the guidance of your inner artist creative spirit. Don't risk silencing your inner artist spirit by romancing the hornet's nest of fear.

The Stages of Rejection in Action

Here's what happened to me. I wanted an art show and I got one. I also got some things that sometimes come along with an art show, which sent me into a state of fear.

Stage 1: My fear was getting a bad review, which I got.

It didn't matter that I sold art from that show; my ego was hurt and it kicked my fear in the butt and sent it in to pester me. I took it personally and didn't paint for a year and a half. "Boo-hoo-hoo! Poor pitiful me," I cried. I thought, *You suck at being an artist!* So, long after everyone forgot about it, I was still hurt and carrying resentment, which bothered me!

Stage 2: However, I carried on and had more art shows. But lo and behold, it happened again! This time in a nationally distributed paper.

However I realized I was doing what I loved, making art, and the critic had only seen my art in a magazine and not in real life. The review was in print and was in the trash by the end of the day, so it didn't really matter much. I got it and it didn't bother me. Besides I made the papers!

Stage 3: I listened to the critic who said my paintings looked too bright and had too much purple in them. I didn't personally know the critic and haven't met the critic to this day. I decided to take action and turn the criticism into something better.

Stage 4: I got it and quieted my ego and fear then turned it to my advantage.

I made a decision to have fun with it! I got into action and made the biggest, brightest, most beautiful purple painting I could think of and happily sold it for the highest price ever. I was happy and satisfied traveling to the bank, still feeling very grateful inside for the tip from the critic now easily paying my rent for an entire year. I got it, took action and had fun with it by being me naturally!

Getting to the core of fear comes through different experiences; many people have different forms of fear. Some have fear of success; some have fear of failure, fear of acceptance, fear of being looked down upon, fear of approval, fear of losing income or fear of losing life. Most of our fears are completely ridiculous.

A good exercise to do when you're in the grips of fear is to ask yourself if your fear is true and if you are absolutely certain it's true. Many artists are starving to death emotionally because they are told that will literally happen to them. I do not know anyone, including myself, who has been to the funeral of an artist who starved to death from pursuing art. However, I have met many who are miserable zombies because they aren't pursuing their art.

We sometimes use fear as the ultimate excuse and scapegoat because we are comfortable just where we are. The ego's favorite trip to take is to be comfy cozy with fear and stay static. Fear that is not instinctual is just a bad repetitive thought pattern that when continuously nourished becomes a nasty habit. If this sounds familiar you can change that. Switch your thoughts, reverse what you are saying, find and focus your passion and your truth and separate those two rascals, fear and ego. When they kick-up their scare tactics at the same time, your artist intuition will gently whisper for you to go another way with opposite thoughts. Ask your inner artist for guidance when fear and ego start shacking up and ruining the neighborhood.

Think of it this way. My fearful ego perceived the bad review I got as a personal rejection; it wasn't. Once I realized that, I got back in the game. Persistence on the road to success is really a numbers game! With every rejection or NO that you receive, you're that much closer to your YES. This is why it's good to keep track of your progress, so you can see hard evidence that the Yes's do indeed happen.

I turned fearful bitterness into sweet abundance by transforming what could have been a devastating resentment into a financial advantage! To this day my paintings are brighter and more vivid than ever. That's indeed what I'm most known for as a painter! I am grateful for that critic and the review. It gave me the motivation to take action on quieting my fears! I let go of the bad story, realized that it wasn't me; it was just a story (someone else' story) and Cha-Ching! I began to thrive.

What is the treasure *you* seek? Have you started to prepare mentally to receive it? Do you have the correct tools to access it? You deserve to have the very best life. No one has a monopoly on truth, most certainly not on yours. What is your truth and what are you doing to live it, critics or not? Are you starting to get the Big Picture? A big, bright purple and yellow one? Well, okay! You can tone it down to your liking.

Chapter Six's Studio Play Sheet

Answer the following questions:

What is the treasure I seek?
What are some things I fear in accomplishing my future Big Picture?
Are the fears that I have real?
Do my fears make me angry?
Where do my fears come from?
Are these fears based on someone else's story, for which I have taken ownership?
What can I do to turn those fears around?
If I didn't have these fears, how would it feel inside?
Could I let these fears go?
If I weren't so afraid, what would I do? I would_____.
What is one thing can I do now to turn them around into success?

TURN YOUR FEARS INSIDE OUT

Next, make a statement for each fear and turn it around and inside out by making it into a positive affirmation and statement.

An example might be: I am afraid that if I do this thing which I want very much, the worst will happen- I'll go broke and people will make fun of me.

Turn that inside out and around by stating: I know the best will happen; it always does. I am already prosperous and I am fun too! People love me. Watch me go!

Do you find it impossible for two different feelings to occupy the same place at the same time? Have you ever noticed that when you're creating a happy and joyful experience, fear and joy cannot exist? Apply your joy of making art into the same joy of telling and selling it.

Invest in yourself here and ask again, *If I weren't so afraid what would I do? Would I seek a mentor or ask other experts how to do something?*

The possibilities of making a living as an artist are endless. Start quieting down the ego's critical false and flimsy cheerleading pep rally made of heavy fear and get into light, joyful one of your true artist spirit. Judgment attracts judgment, criticism attracts criticism and joy attracts joy. The benefits of being a joyful artist outweigh all else.

Ask your artist spirit for guidance; it is alive and well and is always patiently waiting for you to access it.

Creative Activity Points

Learn how to meet other people's needs with your art without neglecting your own needs. Be joyful and full of love for your art.

Your fears are only a lack of love and usually untrue. Life feels much better when you let them go and focus on the Big Picture that you really want and love.

If your ego is kicking up and being fearful and messing up your day-to-day business, you have to sit it down and thank it for its useful information. However, you need to let all disruptive employees go. Fire your ego and send it on a permanent vacation. It deserves it.

Leave anger out of your safe place; don't bring anger to the business table and don't bring anger home.

Consistent actions in business practices send messages to your customers. Be sure you are sending the right messages to the world.

Customers love being around joyful places of business.

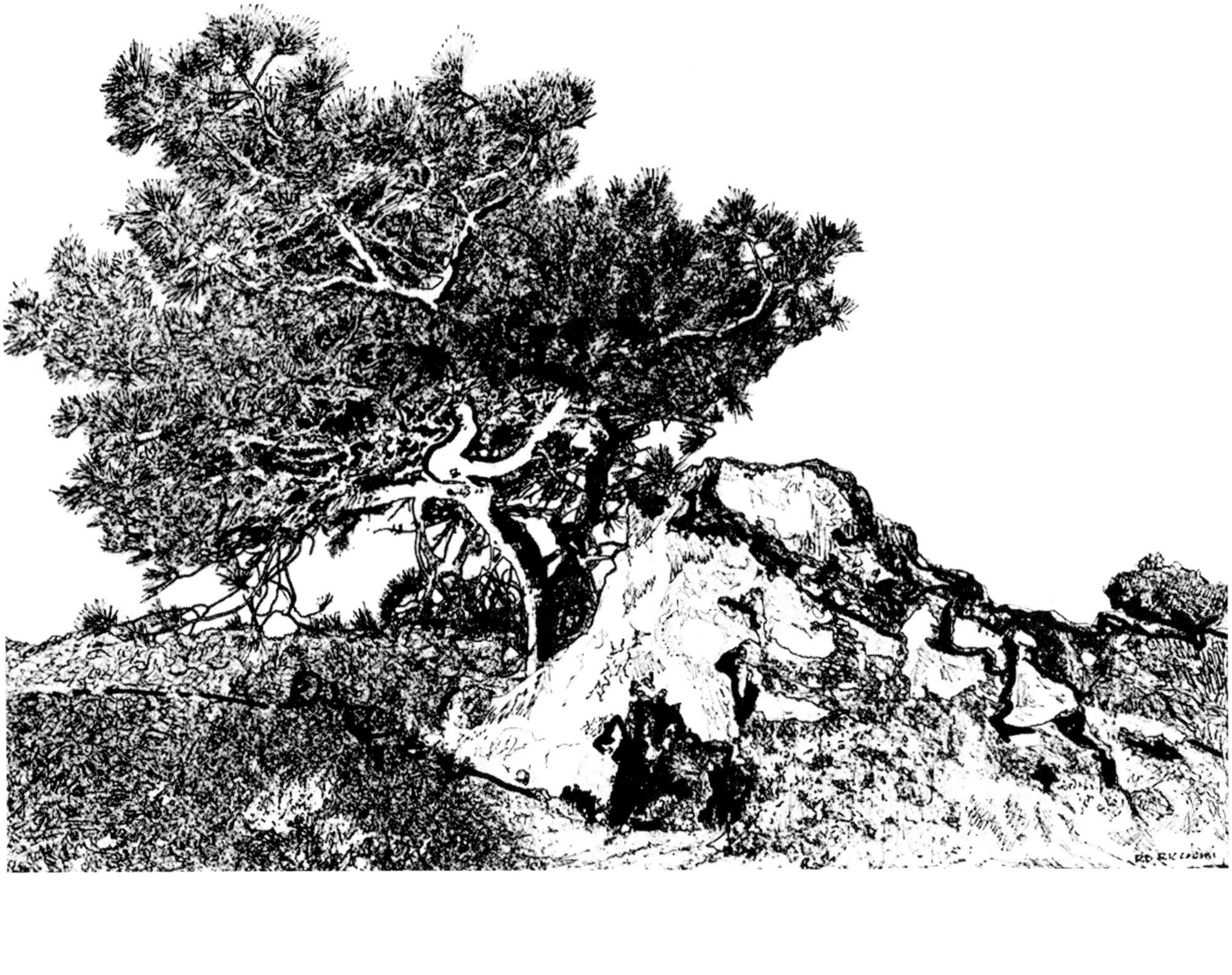

STUDIO THREE
Focus on Gratitude and Appreciation

Step Three: Broadcast Inner Gratitude.

"I have not failed. I've just found 10,000 ways that won't work."
—Thomas Alva Edison (Speaking of the light bulb)

CHAPTER SEVEN

Switch Failure Into Opportunity

Every failure is an invitation for gratitude and change.

LOOK FOR SOLUTIONS

Now, instead of looking back and dwelling on the past, what if we could turn that around? Let's look ahead into the future. We tend to look backwards at failure and sometimes wear it as a badge or some sort of dramatic award for how we were victimized. We waste our time and the time of everyone else who will listen. Remember energy? It's the stuff of which everything is made.

Create good energy by taking risks with common sense and a YES attitude. Think about a specific problem in a new and brilliant way. Stretch it in a good way. A problem can't exist without a solution. I know it sounds wacky but it's true: taking a risk at solving a problem can be quite a positive thing! Thomas Edison failed more than 1,000 times when trying to create the light bulb". (The story is often told as 5,000 or 10,000 times depending on the version.) When asked about it, Edison allegedly said, "I have not failed 1,000 times. I have discovered 1,000 ways to NOT make a light bulb." Look at Mr. Edison's light bulb he did not focus on the failures. Be solution oriented.

Wouldn't it be nice if you could switch the focus of your thoughts, zeroing in on the future you truly want? Would you like to inspire others, have fun on the journey and become successful in the process? That's part of my story. In the best-selling book Manifest Success, I share how I became a professional and successful artist. I talk about when I was consciously unaware how my thinking attracted both good and bad situations. With fine-tuning, dedication and practice, I was able to overcome major difficulties, from poor heath to financial difficulties. I could then focus on the positive aspects of what I wanted to do, paint pictures and live the life of my dreams. I am so grateful I got it!

When you're creating as an artist, you're experimenting with taking positive risks. Life is full of them! You can have a thousand flops; you can create mud and darkness, or light and brilliance in what you make. So what?! It only takes one success to get you into that art show from which you can build.

As adults on the road to reaching our artistic endeavors, most of us are still acting like kids in the back seat of our parent's car asking, "Are we there yet?" Except now you're driving. It just might be time to take a U-turn and stop backseat complaining. The few adults that stay on board for the ride and focus on their prize, whether it's the museum show, the book deal or the Oscar, usually achieve their goal. Admittedly, they are few and far between because so many just gave up. Persistence pays off for the few that stay the course.

Success Begins With Systems

To get where you need to be in the business of art you will need a system. Perhaps a new system that has not yet been invented or one that has been invented but not applied to your vocation. Everyone has a system and most may not even know it. It is the way you do business. We live by and use our own systems, as well as the systems of others. To do our daily routine we must have systems in place. When one doesn't work we simply innovate until we are comfortable. When the electricity goes out, we find another way to do what we need to do. When the car breaks down, we find other forms of transportation. We come up with a new way to take care of our business instead of relying on malfunctioning systems. There's absolutely no reason you can't apply this to your art.

Be open-minded while creating your business system. Listen to what your patrons, customers and community are asking for. You will have to learn to listen and translate. In other words, if they are complaining about something, then the opposite is often the solution and you can then use your talent to create the product they want and need.

Look for innovative ways to get your art out there to the public, your customers. Copy, emulate and study other experts if need be and add your special twist, your special ingredient, with a dash of your expertise and go for it! As you develop your system continue to stretch and reach as you go along. When you get too comfortable, you may stagnate and wonder what happened when no one shows up to purchase your art.

Art Show Example

I created a system in my art business by listening to what people were saying about art and then putting myself in their shoes. An example- At one show, all the artists were all saying "make the paintings bigger!" So we did. The customers came to the shows with ooh's and ah's, stroking our egos. Meanwhile, no one bought except for an occasional bite here and there. What people *were* saying was, "I'd buy that if I could fit it in my house" or "My new house is all windows" and "gorgeous painting, however, I don't live in your country. Do you have a print of it?" The artists and the galleries were all saying make it bigger, frame it differently, hang them differently, lower the prices, make note cards, and on and on. This was all contrary to what the customer was asking for. Can you translate what they wanted? Everyone was trying to translate but they couldn't hear the customer because they were stuck in their old system and refused to modify them. The pictures were already too big to hang in their homes! The potential customers wanted smaller art. They didn't say less expensive or bigger. What they were saying was exactly what they wanted to purchase: smaller original art that would fit on a wall space in a home or office full of windows. They wanted art that could easily be moved and taken with them immediately.

I saw my artist/gallery counterparts scrambling, frustrated, and blaming one another, the audience, the venue, the organizer and finally, each other. By trying to please others, you encourage the distorted idea that someone else, such as a critic or gallery, is responsible for your happiness, which in the long run, takes the artist's power away and makes them uncreative and unhappy. Be careful! Pleasing turns into blaming and before you know it beckons fear and anger out of hiatus.

The harder the artist tries to make others happy, the unhappier they become. Are you dependent upon the behavior of others, of which you have no control rather than creating art? Instead, stick to what you love to create and tell folks about it. This is where you do have complete control.

As I listened to the concerns of other art businesspersons at shows and exhibits, it became apparent that I heard something they didn't. I spoke with the folks who at one time I had thought were in charge of my art career, shared new ideas and offered some suggestions. My overactive ego winced when those suggestions got scoffed at.

All Systems Go!

However, now I feel differently. I changed my artist destiny attitude, took charge and became responsible for my art and myself. With grace, I quietly went in my own business direction, implementing my very own suggestions and quadrupled my income the first year! I did research and found the best way to create a system for what the customer wanted. I then started creating smaller paintings of my art, which were more cost effective to create and reproduce as well. When someone wanted a larger piece of artwork, I could replicate it now from the small one, not the other way around. I now like to say, "All systems go!" and then I go for it.

I soon realized my art was producing more income than my day job, so I quit it. I have continued to thrive and prosper with my art every day since. Listen to your audience who loves you and hear what they are telling you. Find out what they want, where they want to buy it and how they need it delivered. Then, solve their problems with innovation and use your art and today's technology to do so. You don't have to compromise the integrity of your art because what you are changing is just the way it's delivered. Thomas Edison didn't change light; he changed the system. All Systems Go!

Chapter Seven's Studio Play Sheet

Are you digging for gold everywhere but throwing away the overlooked diamonds in the dirt? Are you stuck on one ultimate and golden answer, labeled your Big Picture?

Think of a past failure(s) that turned out to be a blessing in disguise, for which you are now grateful. Write it/them down.

Think of all the world's inventions that came about because of problems and failed experiments. It's really astounding when you study this.

Look around you right now and list ten things that were invented because a problem needed to be solved.

1.

2.

3.

4.

5.

6.

7.

8.

9.

10.

One of the problems you may be facing within yourself is that you are a beginner at this art business part and have no idea where to start. Instead of letting that fear hold you back, consider some suggestions below to help you. Here's a good two-part process to follow:

1. Make a close connection with people who know what they are talking about and follow their lead.
2. Study more about what you want in that field. Dedicate time each day to study on the topics that will move you forward.
3. Don't worry, or care about what other people think about your stuff. This is the recipe for no regrets.

Then the next steps in the process are:

4. Get good leads for your art sales. Let bad ones go.
5. Know what to say to those leads in person or via correspondence.
6. Train people to do the first two objectives on this list.
7. Commit to doing more of #4-6. That's how you grow your art business.

No matter what happened yesterday and what way it went, today is a new day and you can work wonders with that. It's time to rise and shine.

Never discuss your not-yet- achieved successes with artists or other businesspersons less successful than you, including your sales partners and staff. They can only advise you on similar failed circumstances. Let's face it; if they knew the answer, they would be doing it. Seek advice from those who have been there and have real insight. Seek a mentor and be a mentor.

Just like making your art, the more you explore the business side and the more energy you put into it, the more you will get out of it.

Creative Activity Points

Listen for the answer to your audience's problem; that's where your gold mine is. Get your answers and use your art (and others people's systems) to create your financial freedom and create more than art. Create jobs for you and others.

Life is full of contradictions and yet, there can be two right answers. Be open-minded and go in the direction where you feel the love of your Big Picture. Loving what you do is your most powerful tool in your art studio.

Keep good records; separate personal records from business records.

With knowledge comes wisdom. Wisdom + Action = Wealthy Smart Artist

CHAPTER EIGHT

Love Yourself and Others

"Don't let anyone steal your dream. It's your dream, not theirs." —Dan Zadra
Tend to all your relationships. Surround yourself with love and support.

Mind The News

We live in a media-drenched world and when something goes wrong, everybody knows it. Let's face it; bad news travels fast. Today with social networks everyone has the potential to become a worldwide news spokesperson. Be careful what you broadcast. Your cell phone, laptop, computer device are basically a news station capable of linking up with various networks all over the globe within seconds. The art world network is no different and, in fact any news in the art world can make or break your career fast. News is addictive so be sure keep your news good!

Did you ever play the game "telephone" as a kid? We sat in a circle and whispered into the ear of our friend sitting beside us? The game players whispered the message to the next person around the room and so on it went until it reached the last person in the circle. Then, the last person announced the message to everyone. Sometimes it was the same message but most times it became something entirely different. The room howled with laughter. Today's technology has resurrected this game and it has run rampant.

Injury and Intuitive Nudges

I remember a few years back, I experienced my own version of telephone. Before the days of the Internet and social marketing, I had an injury and was debilitated for a while. It gave me time to think about life and realize I truly was an artist. It was my passion. While healing physically and mentally I received gentle intuitive nudges. It was as though I was being prepared at a new level in my heart for the wonderful and artistic career I desired. When I felt better, I traveled cross-country to visit and relax with good friends. It was just what I needed. They invited me to an art show where I might run into some folks I knew. *How fun*, I thought. *I'm back in the swing of things!*

As soon as we arrived, I saw the familiar face of another gallery director. I waved and he turned white as if he'd seen a ghost. The first thing out of his mouth was, "Thank God! I heard you were dead!" Now, mind you I had only been out of commission for a few months and I had no idea who told who in the telephone circle about me. My sabbatical from the world led to the apparent news of my demise. In the days of landline telephone, you could have a cold in New York and by the time the news traveled to the west coast, you would have been reported mysteriously dead and buried two hours later in Los Angeles. That was then; today's news is viral and travels even faster.

Which Messenger Will you be?

With that said, do you continue this cycle of being the bearer of bad news, the Angel of Darkness? When someone does something right or brings you good news, tell them that it is great news! Share the good news. Positive messages will produce greater results. Start to say WOW! more often; express it when someone says something positive.

When someone says something negative, you might say it is an interesting viewpoint but then be on your way. Don't reward negativity and discard positivity. If someone looks great, compliment them; if they have a clever idea, support them. Negativity only supports the starving artists in all of us. Positivity supports excellence, genius and the brilliant master artist energy in all of us.

Practice Positive Action and Associations

Draw the line and take control of your life. Make a decision to start doing something good that you have developed through repetition or something you'd like to try. Develop clear goals and objectives. Practice asking yourself, "How could I make this situation better?" And, take action immediately, which means doing something every day that moves you toward your goal of living your ideal life. Stop repeating the habits that do not serve you in good ways. You deserve the very best life ever!

Friendships and associations, speech and thought are all tied together. You have a basic human need to belong; humans are social creatures and this need actually drives us, as we are all connected by energy. However, you must find balance and supportive friendships and relationships that build you up rather than tear you down. You need a place to be yourself, be appreciated, valued and honored. Find surroundings where you can develop yourself happily and comfortably while being your true self. Model this for others. If you choose to bring your best artwork out into the light, you must do the same thing with your friends and associations. Can you proudly bring them out into the light as well?

It's often said, "Birds of a feather flock together." So, are you guilty by association? Do you involve yourself in nitpicking, gossiping, complaining, and sitting around talking about the same old biased opinions over and over again? If you think that next time will be different, think again. It never is because doing the same thing over and over and expecting different outcomes is a huge waste of time and just plain crazy. Did you ever pass by or sit next to a table of so-called "friends" talking about what's wrong with everything, nay saying with judgments, resentments, and complaints? Have you done this too and chimed in yourself? I call this the DRAMA-NAY-TRICKS effect. If feeds on itself in a never-ending drama loop and blocks your channel to your higher artist self.

You get together with friends, with good intentions of course, and then take an emotional dump all over them or them on you. "I was tricked! How did that happen again?" Do you let your friends do that to you? And then, do you comfort them? How does that contribute to anyone having a joyful life? How does that contribute to you having a joyous experience? If this is you, you may want to take some time to reflect on why you have a need to participate in this type of dramatic activity. What is the one major and glaring thing you have in common with these upsetting or repetitive situations? It is that you are in them. It's habitual and perpetuating. It's time to knock it off. Just because you can gossip doesn't mean you should be involved in this sort of psychological infection. There are entire twelve-step programs dedicated to this type of nonproductive, codependent behavior.

Drama-Nay-Tricks Syndrome

Since the true nature of your artist heart is designed to care and support others through sharing your gift, you can become addicted to drama without realizing what's happening. I have seen this in artists, out and about in the community as well as in many art organizations and clubs. You think you can help these unaware zombies and vampires with your noble good examples and justify it by saying it builds character. Perhaps, but why put yourself through that? Life quickly becomes unbalanced, bogged down in an over-care symphony and like vampires and zombies, our artist heart shuts down in the presence of the DRAMA-NAY-TRICKS effect. Don't forget, we're all actors in our own play. You get to direct, produce and star in your own movie called "life." Why then do you sometimes become so unaware of potential results as you show up at a bon fire dressed in gasoline-soaked underwear? Instead of that Academy Award you secretly expected, all you get is a big, bad hurtful explosion! Over-caring and score keeping, besides being exhausting, come with a price. Resentment builds in your drama circle. The listeners start being viewed as smothering goodie-goodies. Vampire and zombie cronies will usually lash out in fear, attacking others for being unsupportive. The listeners swoop in to clean up the mess, save the day and start the drama circle all over again.

Gossiping and participating in judgmental stories feeds the ego's know-it-all hunger but it does something else too. It creates internal conflict. Conflict creates stress and stress creates aging. Peace is ageless. Learn how to be at peace. Peace is your anti-aging secret weapon.

You can spend a lifetime doing this by joining clubs, signing anti-this-and-that petitions, being a part of social media network sites, perpetuating more and more drama, complaining about your woes to anyone bored enough to listen. Or, you can set a good example by spending a few hours a week mastering positive solutions, listening to the right mentor, studying and practicing. Success takes sacrifice, not over-caring. The first thing to sacrifice is complaining! Nothing hurts or bothers you when you're appreciating things. Could you let go and release complaining?

The Good News

The good news is that with practice and consistency you can become aware of your own connection with your thoughts and feelings. The thing most people don't understand is that to a degree you control your thoughts and feelings simply because you choose the thoughts you think. Most of the time the way you feel about your art career depends upon the nature of your thoughts. Much frustration comes from thinking that all you can control are the outside circumstances and people around you, which you cannot. But the really good news is that once you're aware that you can change your thoughts, as well as the environment where you hang out, you realize that you really are in control of most everything on in your life. Complaining cannot exist next to gratitude or appreciation. Those complainers are true angels, uncut diamonds in the rough pointing you in another direction.

Learn how to balance your personal energy, thoughts and feelings that you send out into the world. They come back to you, for sure. Deep subconscious stores of judgment and resentment are counter-productive to self-empowerment and health and simply do not resonate with your higher self or with others on your journey.

When you are tempted to complain about something, stop for 30 seconds, calm down and ask, "What can I do to make the situation better?" When you first meet someone wait a few seconds before judging. People tend to pass judgment in a blink of an eye for no reason. If someone does bring something negative to the conversation, consider being quiet or speak only of improving the situation through appreciation. Your associations with either follow you or they won't. What's important is where you want to be. The more you do this, the less the social vampires and zombies will want to associate with you. Thank God for these bitter brothers and sour sisters for they bring us vital information. They show us, in no uncertain terms, where we do not want to be.

We are extensions of the people we hang out with, the movies we see, the books we read and the TV shows we watch. If you continue to allow yourself to be in a complaining, problem-laden, poverty-ridden conscious group then you deserve to be there. It's your right and choice to remain wherever you are. However, you can move yourself out of that space into a less burdensome environment at anytime. Do you want to allow for success or failure? It's your choice. You don't have to walk out on anybody in your life but think about seeking out friends who are making positive, ambitious and enthusiastic things happen in their lives. Are the people you choose to hang out doing what you want to do, being what you want to be and living the way you want to live?

Anger, Guilt and Resentment

Are you angry? Anger ruins your health. Release anger. Anger is an outside-yourself energy that ruins everything it touches including your health, your relationships and your career.

If you have a tendency to get angry, make up your mind today that you will investigate every possible way to release its grip on your life.

Like anger, there is no room for guilt or resentment in any business. Guilt is a past regret about you and resentment is about someone else. They are both destructive and will block your artistic success. It is always good to investigate any lingering resentments or guilt regarding the past. Don't forget to look at possible harsh feelings directed toward everything from other business entities to organizations. I have witnessed many folks in the arts harboring resentments and guilt regarding places and organizations from the past that they had associations with. Guess what? Those places, organizations and entities have no clue these resentments exist! What a waste of precious time.

Change Your Vibration

If you don't like what's going on in your life, you've got to make a decision!

Sacrifice complaining and be aware, pay attention, let go of past resentment and look for the magic that is being revealed to you through appreciation. It's time to grow up and leave the pity party; the food is no good for you there. Remember, as we mentioned earlier, if you let external things bother you, you are setting yourself up for that vibration, which impacts what it is being attracted back to you.

If you don't like what you're experiencing you have to change your vibration. What we read, speak, see and hear sets up your vibration. Remember, we are an energy field always vibrating.

Sometimes energy gets stuck and you may need to work with a professional to clear out old energetic patterns. Unhealthy ties to people, places and events can keep you trapped in a revolving door of disappointment and pain.

Methods of Clearing Old Energy

There are many processes to help with this including therapy and counseling. Space clearing is a way to cleanse and clear the energy of buildings.

However, for a more profound and swift alternative method, I like energetic cord cutting. It is a fascinating and effective energy release process that my close friend and energy-aficionado,

Connie Stewart, at Soul-Sync Consulting professionally assists people with from every walk of life. She says the following about space clearing:

"Environments are energetically patterned by how people use the spaces. Rooms do not become empty just because people leave them physically. Places are affected by human psychophysical energies. These energetic patterns remain in the subtle field of the environment even after we physically leave a place and can affect how a particular space feels. This pattern of energy has a subtle form and structure to it and can have a toxic effect on an individual if the energy is particularly chaotic and negative.

A space clearing session can clear the effect of disharmonious energies and noxious thought emanations. Removing these energies can erase constricting conditions, allowing for a freer, fresher participation in that environment. This clearing eliminates tensions and promotes a more healthy and productive milieu. With a space clearing session, the entire environment will take on a brighter, lighter and clearer quality. People often comment on how much the place feels as though a breeze of fresh air has cleared the space and that it's easier to breath!"

On the energetic cord cutting process, Connie tells us:

"The ceremony of "Cord Cutting" is based on the premise that when we enter into relationship with a person or even business relationships, and contracts of all sorts, an energetic thread or cord is activated. As we move through life, often these relationships no longer are what we need or want them to be. "Cord Cutting" allows for the energetic thread that has been running to be cut. Relationships don't have to end, but this allows for new beginnings instead of being trapped in the past. Sometimes, we want relationships to end, such as when you are no longer in a relationship with a lover. Every time you enter into such a relationship, particularly one that leads to sexual involvement, an energetic thread is started. If the relationship continues, the thread gets stronger. Often, people can feel this or have an intuitive sense of what is going on with their partner. This is due to the energetic connection. Even in relationships that have ended, years later, there still can be a tapping in."

If this type of professional work doesn't call to you, then you could be of great benefit for you to start to clear your attitude and space on your own immediately. When you try to justify where you are by pointing out how bad things are, you amplify the situation through your attention to it and are headed in the wrong direction. Switch your thought to one that feels hopeful. Begin appreciating what's in front of you and take notice of what begins to happen. The good stuff starts coming in!

There are many more positive things being attracted into your life than negative. While negative things appear more memorable focus on all the good things you attract around you every day.

The funny thing is that none of those negative stories we tell or become accomplices to, are us. They're not who we are. They are just stories. Nothing is too good to be true. Don't let the naysayers hamper your abilities. Set your sights high and expect the best of yourself and others. Wake up right now, not tomorrow or some other time down the road. There is a magnificent life waiting for you. Release your tight hold on old stories, especially the starving artist saga.

You create your circumstances by how you honor and value your artist self worth.

The second the artist settles for less than they deserve, guess what happens? They get even less than they would have settled for! That is not making a living with your art; that's crazy! Begin right now to honor and value your artistic worth.

There will always be people in recession; there will always be struggling artists, there will always be people prospering and there will always be artists thriving. Make a decision that honors the way you prefer to live and determine to stick with it. Create your thriving artist living and all circumstances in life by how you honor and value your artist self!

Trust your heart, intuition and instincts - they are your best life guides; they are pure. Your mind is powerful beyond measure - use it responsibly. No matter where you are or who you are around, feed your mind positive information daily.

Gift of the Present

When I'm driving in my car, I have fun staying in the moment by looking at trees, houses, people, and how the sun creates amazing shadows to name a few. Sometimes when something negative from the past or fear of the future is in my head and it's not leaving me, I actually have to start saying to myself..."there's a green sign"…"the mailbox has a 30 on it" and before you know it I receive a gift...I'm back in the moment.

Like a master artist with their Big Picture, always keep yourself, friendships and the things you do, in love's highest light by honoring and valuing your time and worth.

Live magnificently and become calmly observant by appreciating your surroundings. The same energy that flows through you flows through everything in the Universe. You are part of everyone and everyone is part of you; we are all breathing the same air. Your Journey is not meant to be alone; know your oneness with all that is, and chose your traveling companions wisely. We are all connected through love and the strongest of us show love for all things. With an unstoppable attitude and a collaborating team of like-minded co-creators you can resolve and accomplish anything! That's what I call manifesting a successful Big Picture!

Chapter Eight's Studio Play Sheet

Apart from your family, name the five people with whom you spend the most time:

1.

2.

3.

4.

5.

Make a list of all the positive qualities of your friends.
Are they kind to themselves and others?
What do they have in common?
Are your friendships nurturing or draining?
Do you speak of each other's success and genuinely want everyone to succeed?
Do they laugh a lot?
Do you speak of abundance to each other or proliferate stories of lack?
Are you open to others' input, allowing you to look beyond your own points of view about The Big Picture?
Do your friends honor your time and worth or dump all their problems on you?
Do you honor your friend's time and worth or dump all your problems on them?
Do you feel uplifted and inspired or drained and exhausted after spending time with your friends and associates?
Do you see yourself as your source of abundance or view others as your source of abundance?
Do your friends, associates and associations contribute to your betterment?
Do you have trusted advisors whose opinions you trust and honor?
Can you let go of negative feedback and give positive feedback in appreciation of yourself and others?

BIG PICTURE WHAT YOU WANT EXERCISE #1

Think of a person or situation that you are angry with. Now, spend the next few minutes writing out a statement of how YOU WANT the situation to be. It can start with, "I would like... or wouldn't it be nice if we" Remember, you are describing what YOU WANT or WISH the person or situation to be, NOT how you DON'T WANT IT TO BE, but how YOU WANT IT TO BE.

Take in details of your conversations and surroundings with your head and heart and ask questions if your inner gut ask for more information.

Ask questions, take classes and learn about areas in your life where you need more clarity.

Ask advice from trusted friends, therapists and professional experts.

Take regular quiet time outs to review and digest what you have learned or taken in.

Learn to develop and refine your reason skills and see the true spirit in yourself and others; enjoy your beautiful, bright spirit and let it shine.

If you were putting a dream team together to create a phenomenal accomplishment, who would it consist of?

Feed yourself positive information daily; drop old stories, as they are not what you want.

Make a list of your values and read them often.

Professional Etiquette

Before going on a gallery exhibition site or future art customer appointment, call to verify and tell your prospective customer how much time you will need for your art presentation. Show up on time, not early, not late. When you arrive, verify the agreed upon time they have set aside. Take up no more time than agreed to. Leave with a decision being made about your art career, show or sale in writing. Have each other's contact information and a new time for your next meeting, if appropriate. Always keep your professional word. You will make a lasting and respectful impression as an efficient person that won't waste their time and more importantly, your time. Be clear.

Like most vendors, galleries generate more business by focusing time and energy on strong and independent artists. They want artists who are at peace instead of the indecisive in their stable of brilliance. Guess which artists make the most income?

Follow the Golden Rule with yourself and others. The Golden Rule not only applies to how we treat others ethically, it also applies to how we treat ourselves.

You can't be neutral on your Big Picture, you're either moving closer to it or farther away. Don't let fear into your house, gallery, mind or story. Everything counts in getting you closer to The Big Picture and you may have to give up some things in your life story to get there. This includes actions you take, where and how you live and conversations you have. Be clear on the real you here and now.

Creative Activity Points

Do business with people who are positive, lift the spirits of others and are problem solvers.

Should you end a professional relationship, always be gracious and remove your art smoothly, promptly and professionally. Leave drama alone.

When looking for a potential place to do business, never show up at a gallery, future customer's place of business or private space uninvited or unannounced. Always, always have an appointment. Burn this into your mind.

New travels fast; bad news travels faster. Think twice before you broadcast (in person and through social technology) to the world.

If your life is out of balance, chances are your checkbook is too.

Some persons can only make conversation through complaining. Never speak ill or bad of other persons in business, including other artists or galleries. Let your light shine brightly and stay clear of that sort of thing.

Be at peace. Peace is ageless. Peace is your anti-aging secret weapon.

Put a dream team together of trusted advisors who are positive, upbeat and successful.

Always speak of abundance and prosperity, yours and others.

Keep all appointments; confirm and reconfirm them On appointments, take up no more time than agreed to.

Leave appointments with a decision being made in writing about your art, show or sale.

Always be sure your business appointments have each other's contact information and a new time for your next meeting when necessary.

Ask if you are understood and be clear with your mutual agreements as to logistics and who is responsible for what.

Always keep your word professionally and personally.

If you cannot follow through on your agreement and commitments for some reason, you MUST immediately get in touch with your business contact to reschedule.

Honor and value your artist self worth and that of others as well.

Follow the Golden Rule with yourself and others.

While you can pick up on and read the energy of others, other persons pick up yours as well. Only transmit the type of energy that is productive to all. What comes around goes around!

Business grows where integrity flows.

CHAPTER NINE

Turn A Failure into Opportunity and Discover Your Goldmine

"There is absolutely nothing that separates the elite from the paupers except their expectations. If you wish to rise above the masses, then let the fire burn fiercely within you. Do this and it shall be done!"
—J. Arthur Holcombe, Author of *The Path of Truth and Courage*

Your art is much like a goldmine waiting to be discovered! You could be so close to that goldmine that you might not even know it. The way to know where your gold is located is by first knowing what your passions are. We have been exploring and discovering your passions all through The Big Picture. Have you been keeping track? When you uncover passions and apply, your art you will uncover your gold. Set the stage for success. Visualize it and then suit up and show up!

In the 1800s in the small town of Julian, California, there was a gold rush. There is a famous goldmine there that made a local man very rich. This man bought the goldmine from another man who failed to continue digging. The other man said there was no gold in the mountain. The next man who bought the mine had vision and was passionate about digging and knew that he would find it through persistence. He decided to dig just a few feet from where the defeated man dug. That is where he struck gold. He later became the mayor of San Diego and the governor of California. Today you can see his beautiful Victorian mansion near historic Balboa Park in San Diego, California because he knew where his passion was. Mr. Waterman took a failure and changed it to an opportunity and eventually bought his dream house on First Avenue.

Your vision is the ability to see a goldmine where others do not. When I opened my gallery in Old Town San Diego, many burned out retailers told me that the place had seen its hay-day and that people no longer went there to shop. Well, maybe shoppers didn't go there anymore or perhaps potential customers did indeed go there and those disgruntled business owners could no longer see them because of their attitudes regarding changes that they could not adapt to. What an interesting concept indeed!

I saw a potential gold mine where others said the well was dry. I made a business plan, took baby steps and got my foot in the door. Each year since making the decision to go forward, my business has doubled and my location has also increased in size. While other beautiful galleries have closed up shop around us declaring that art is dead in this town, our gallery is thriving. People are buying art, everyday in fact, business is fantastic and the place is a goldmine. Why is it so? It has to do with our attitude, our systems, common sense, persistence and vision.

There is a very thin line between getting - and not getting - what you want. I see this all the time. Artists of all sorts just simply give up when they are just within reach of their gold.

You can only turn failure around for yourself. You can't do that for others. You can set an example but we each have to turn failure around for ourselves. Another can hold the door of opportunity open for you. However, only you can walk through it. You must discover, and want your gold first before others can see it. That light of passion you begin to shine by doing so will attract others to your career.

Manage Your Goldmine

The financial numbers always leave clues to your goldmine. When your art generates income, that money must be managed separately from your personal finances area. It is a good practice to do this. These numbers are the clues that are your treasure map to your gold mine.

Seeing your numbers and the results of them indicates where to build a life of your dreams and keeping track of it to see what's going on with your mine and if you are in the right place with it. This way you can monitor your business progress and prepare yourself for opportunities. For example, you can see if your receipts are taxable or non-taxable income; you can see your expenses and where your money is going. Keep records of your travel, including mileage. Ask your accountant what to do right now, not at the end of tax season. It will make life easier when you pay your taxes at the end of the year. Ask the accounting firm exactly how they want your files set up and then do it that way from now on. The less time your accountant spends trying to figure out your mess, the less you pay them for their services.

Keep good records so you can turn them in to your accountant at the end of the year and concentrate on making your art and developing your business. Your art is just the tip your goldmine.

You can earn all the money you'll ever need by providing a service with one great idea put into action. Then, you can go to work to be satisfied. You're magnetizing what you are projecting!

Working versus Earning

Mentally separate the idea in your head that you must work hard to earn money. We are programmed from the time we are infants that we must go to work to earn money. For some reason we interpret this program as something hard to do, tedious and bad, toiling away and wind up doing it.

Do you love your job? Lots of people do and many don't.

Work is made for you. You go to work to do what you love doing for satisfaction. You are not made for work. It gives you a means of expression. You earn money by providing a service of value. That is what earns you money and helps you make a living in art.

Do you love what you're doing for work? Is your work satisfying? Is the service you provide satisfying you creatively? Spend your days doing what you love. Give your all to what you love to do. Provide to others a service of value that you love, that's how you earn money. Separate the idea of working versus earning money.

As we have been learning, your artist business and personal life are magnetic mirrors. How you see yourself is what is mirrored back to you. When you see failure, you get failure; When you see artistic success, you get artist success. Start reflecting back what you want financially, as well, with this action.

Chapter Nine's Studio Play Sheet

Have you already turned around a perceived failure and had success?

Name a failure that you can turn around for yourself. Start by turning it around into a positive affirmation.

Do this from now on until it becomes a habit of looking at things in a new way.

Example: I'm so broke; I need to cut back to find an extra fifty dollars a month to get by.

Turn this into: I now create an extra fifty dollars (or whatever amount you wish) a month – week –day etc. and I will create this by…. (insert the action you now do to create your monetary wealth). For example: I teach an art class to 5 people once a week at the local community center for $ 25.00 a person.

THE MONEY MIRROR GOLDMINE

Draw a simple stick figure image on a sticky note. This is what financial success as an artist looks like to you. Post it and meditate on the image.

Write on your sticky notes and put them around your mirror. Create affirmations on the sticky notes like: "I save 10% of every paycheck and every art sale". Make another sticky note; write on it- I know and honor my value and worth. On another, write "I attract success and abundance every day into my life because that is who I am. I am prospering everyday as I add to my bank account. The money flows to me in waves of abundance like the air I breathe. I am rich! I am a money magnet. My cash flow is always positive."

See yourself in the middle of the mirror and read the affirmations out loud to yourself as you look into the mirror. Visualize yourself going to the bank and making deposits. Even when paying your bills, say thank you because you are able to pay them. Recall a time when you held a loving puppy or kitten and recapture that feeling as you say your affirmations. Say them aloud while you're in the shower, driving in the car or wherever you have a little private time. Do it until you memorize them and say them automatically. As money comes to you say to yourself with that holding-the-puppy/kitten-feeling we talked about, "Yes! Of course this prosperity comes to me; I am a magnet for prosperity and I am so grateful and happy to receive my windfall." Affirm and re-affirm with loving puppy and kitty thoughts until it becomes your truth.

If you love constructing things, make a real money mirror. Get an old framed mirror and apply your affirming notes in decoupage on it. You can do this fun action project for all sorts of goals you want to manifest!

Creative Activity Points

Are there other business systems that are potential goldmines that can be applied to your art? Instead of reinventing the wheel, purchase or replicate someone else's unused or successful system and apply it to your art business.

Keep good records of all your expenses.

Keep receipts in order in separate file folders, one for each month. Stay organized and clutter free.

Set up your accounting files exactly as your accountant suggests, and continue to organize your record keeping this way so from now on.

Honor and value your worth, both what you can physically see, as well as the untapped riches.

Always be able to see and know your financial Big Picture with ease.

Spend less than you earn. Set out and keep a healthy balance between investing in experiences today and saving for memories of tomorrow.

Have CLEAR financial agreements in business whether you're selling or bartering.

Keep impeccable records and hire an accountant. Be orderly.

Keep your art business finances separate from your personal account with its own business checkbook and savings account.

Keep good records and enter them on a daily basis in a good software accounting program such as QuickBooks from Intuit.

If you have more than one business, keep separate records for each business.

Set up a separate business savings account in which to place your collected sales tax and other projected applicable taxes. To cover your tax obligations, simply transfer money from this savings account into your business checking account when needed. Get this money out of your regular business checking account and Do Not use this money for anything other than paying your taxes. In the meantime, it will be earning interest.

Back-up your computerized financial records to an external storage device or online back-up service on a daily basis!

Back up your art picture computer file records to an external storage device as you create them!

Back up your computer, customer files or any type of computer file; back up on a very regular basis.

CHAPTER TEN

Art Appreciation

"There are people who have money and people who are rich." —Coco Chanel

Money is such a huge obstacle for most folks. They dwell on the lack of money so much, that they actually attract a greater lack. Simply put, like attracts like. It is the law of the Universe.

The best thing to do is to focus on abundance while leaving the money factor out of it. Your desire for money might mess with the vibration you emit in order to attract the abundance you desire. In the western culture, money is so much a part of our everyday life that it can be very hard to wrap your thinking around leaving it out of your desire for more abundance. You have to become comfortable with money instead of worrying about not having enough. This has been a challenge for me, as well as most artists I have met.

As you read earlier, your subconscious mind cannot tell the difference between what's real and what's imagined! So, in order to create a situation in your mind that is real, you simply need to understand that the more comfortable you are with money, the more of it you attract. The same is true with customers, collectors and business partners. I tell artists that if you have created an exhibit of your very best work at home, completed and ready to hang, you're more likely to attract and magnetize an art show. That great art you have made is the magnet for the show to happen, as well as the customers and business associates that come with it. Having a money magnet in your possession will do the same.

Think about these next questions. If you drew a picture, let's say ink on paper, would it be of any value? If you had in your possession a Rembrandt ink drawing on paper, would it have value to it? Printed money is nothing more than inked paper that's used as a form of energetic appreciation for goods and services. What is the physical difference between a one-dollar bill and a one hundred dollar bill? Not much, but having one in your possession, as opposed to the other, *feels* different. A wealthier, more prosperous feeling is attached to the One Hundred dollar bill based on how we respect value, trust and honor it.

A Wealth Building Exercise

Here's a wealth consciousness building exercise to try. You can do this with printed paper money tucked away in your wallet. You won't actually spend it (unless it's for an emergency and you must.) Use a $50 or $100 bill if you can. To create the sensation of a stack of bills, cut pieces of paper the same size as your $50 or $100 bill and wrap the real one around them. This bundle is not to spend but to take out and feel, touch, and know that you *could* spend. Put it in your pocket, purse or wallet. Next comes the fun part.

When you see something you like or love that's a hundred dollars or less, express to yourself, "I love that and I can afford that!" however don't spend the money in your pocket. What you are doing is sending a message to your subconscious crew a strong message of appreciation that you love that thing and you can afford that thing. YES, you can! It's real. You have the money in your pocket. You can repeat this game everywhere you go! If you did this all day long, mentally you would spends thousands of dollars and send a strong message of appreciation and abundance to your subconscious mind. You can do this with any amount bill: $20, $50, $100, etc. However, don't do this with your debit or credit card as it defeats the purpose. We're talking cash in your pocket here, not plastic credit. So play and say, "I love that and I can afford that!" Do this exercise and see if you notice any changes in your mood, abundance and cash flow.

Know Your Worth (And Overhead!)

In order to keep things in perspective you must value the worth of your time. You must know your cost-of-living overhead. From a business point of view, the artist must know how much it costs in time and supplies to live and create what they do for their art living. When you determine this, you can determine your value. When you budget for your monthly expenses, you must include your art. You know how much you need for rent, mortgage, car payment and you know how much work you have to do to get paid to do take care of that business. Now, add your art supply cost to that. It's all in your overhead expenses, regardless if you open an art business or make art as a hobby.

If you're not good with money, you have to change that and you can! Let's say you budget $100 a month for art supplies. Put $100 in an envelope and use that only for your art supplies. Write the month on the outside of the envelope and make twelve different envelopes, one for each month. As you spend the money, put the receipts along with a list of what you spent the money on, back into the envelope for that month's records. You can see what you're spending the budget on every month. You will need your receipts later for your record keeping.

If you spend it all resist the urge to buy any more art supplies that month. Additionally, don't borrow from next month's art supply budget. If you use that money for something else, you don't buy any art supplies that month. You blew your budget for art supplies that month. Period. This works the same way for everything you budget. If you budget a hundred fifty dollars a month for food and you spend it all, you don't eat. Be responsible to yourself and your art career; think twice before spending monies on frivolous things. When you don't respect and honor your worth why should anyone else!? When you have money left over at the end of the month, put it in your savings and keep your budget at one hundred dollars till you can handle increasing the budget. If the money you make is not cutting it, then create other new sources of income to increase your spending budget.

Sell your art to increase your monthly budget and from the profits, pay yourself 30%. Take 20% of your sales and put it in savings just for your art business, as you'll need it for the future to pay taxes and other bills that will pop up. Take the remaining 50% and re-invest it in your art

What to Charge

How much should you charge for your art? You'll know really fast if you're not making any profit. You know how much to charge your future employer when you ask for a wage at a job. If you don't make enough income there you either get a raise in pay, quit and get a better job or take on another job to make ends meet. The same goes for your art prices; you either quit making it, sell more of it in more places or raise your prices. Check what other professional artists with your experience are charging. If you're still stumped, be realistic and set manageable goals for your pricing. A ridiculous price usually means you don't want to sell your art or you're showing to the wrong crowd. That's okay.

However, never show work you do not want to sell. You can always raise prices but if you need to lower them to sell your art, people will talk about how you must be starving! Gotcha!

When I figured out my costs including my overhead, I had to double the prices of my art to make a profit. Once I adjusted this, I started selling three times as many pieces and items than previously. When I honored and valued my worth more, so did others. Life becomes more manageable when costs are known. Your income increases and your value increases. It's funny how that all works.

Besides keeping excellent financial records, record your life in words, pictures, video, art and memories - not credit card statements. Only use credit for business loans that have a guaranteed return on investment. That's art appreciation!

Have you sacrificed complaining? Your parents gave you life, so what are you doing with it? Complaining about your money hardships? Are you developing yourself as best you can? Your spiritual DNA is perfect. Are you using a good organized study program to better your life? Stop complaining about finances and keep track of them. Know what's going on. If you don't, it's your own fault, no one else's. Do something financially beneficial with your artist life.

Need help pricing your art?

Try these six different steps.

They are:

Decide on the exact amount of earnings you wish to have.

Feel good and worthy of the amount you desire.

Repeat a prosperity affirmation daily until it becomes a habitual way of thinking.

For example: "I am so happy and grateful that I am continuously making my artist living through many avenues. Whether I am working, playing, sleeping I am creating my art." Keep repeating affirmations like this until they become a habit. Write them on sticky notes and place them strategically where you see them.

Next, invest time everyday studying the Law of Compensation. Many notable people have written about this Universal Law, which is basically about the willingness to give it all up in order to have it all. Ralph Waldo Emerson said, "For everything you have missed, you have gained something else; and for everything you gain, you lose something else." He also writes, "The whole of what we know is a system of compensations. Every defect in one manner is made up in another. Every suffering is rewarded; every sacrifice is made up; every debt is paid."

Decide what you are prepared to give in return for the amount of income you have chosen to earn.

Now think, feel and act like the person who is already living the income-producing life that you wish to have.

Let's go over that again.

Decide on the exact amount of earnings you wish to have.

Feel good and worthy of this amount you desire.

Repeat a prosperity affirmation daily until it becomes a habitual way of thinking.

Invest time everyday studying the Law of Compensation.

Decide what you are prepared to give in return for the amount of income you have chosen to earn.

Feel and act everyday like the person who is already earning what you wish to earn.

What can you learn from this lesson?

The 4 Rules of Money

Think of making money as a game and if it's a game, there are rules to the game. If you want to earn money in art or anything else you need know these four things.

Money is an idea and the idea about money is about exchange. Where did money come from? Before money we used to exchange things like animals, food, gold, land, and so forth. One thing exchanged for another. So if you want money to make a living from your art you have to think about what you can provide in exchange for the money. Whether it is your talent, your service, your physical art, information or knowledge, you have to think about how you can offer it to more than one person.

You need to be brutally honest with yourself here and ask, "Is there is a real need for what I have to offer that could be exchanged for money? The good news is each one of us has expertise somewhere with knowledge, educational information or life experience that can be shared in exchange for money.

You have to be good at getting your message out about your service, product or expertise to as many people as possible. This is called marketing your story and sales, which was cover earlier, You do this everyday when you express your ideas, opinions or beliefs.

Hire out the things that aren't your strengths. If you are not good at selling or marketing your art hire someone to help you. You can pay for them to help you or if money is tight, you may consider trading or bartering with them, deferring payment or partnering with them on another project.

TITHING VS. CHARITY GIVING

To allow more money to flow into your life you must also give money back. This is a principle known as tithing. Tithing is ten percent of the gross income you earn. Many people tithe money to their church; however, you can tithe to anything that inspires your artist spirit. When you tithe you create space for more income including money to come back to you. Tithe with gratitude and thanks.

Giving to a charity is not tithing. It is a great thing to do but it is different and when you only give to places that are in need, through the law of attraction you can actually perpetuate and create more ongoing need of never having enough. I suggest giving to something or someone who inspires you with no attachment to your gift.

Chapter Ten's Studio Play sheet

The Everyday Appreciation Game

On your way to work today notice anything that you yourself did not create. Say out loud (or quietly if more appropriate) "WOW!" or "I appreciate that!" Notice after about fifteen minutes how you feel inside.

Repeat after me, "WOW! I appreciate that!"

You have been given a gift called life. Before you start your day, before you turn on the computer, open the e-mails, or turn on the TV, say thank for the things you have in life and the situations that brought these things to you. Do this for a solid fifteen minutes. You can do this quietly if there are a lot of people nearby.

At the start of your day, every day from now on, be thankful for 15 minutes.

How do you open up to hear your true spirit? Celebrate your artist spirit through expressing creativity! Write a poem, paint a picture, take beautiful photography, sing show tunes, or cook a gourmet meal. Appreciate and tap into the authentic artist self which comes through your artistic creation.

What's Going On With Your Goldmine?

How do you know what's going on with your money at a glance?

With accounting software you can create a profit and loss record to see where you stand and you can look at every day. If you don't have software or can't afford it, you're going to have to do this by hand or via a simple excel spread sheet. Look at your profit and losses to evaluate your journey and see if you are indeed on course with creating your Big Picture. When you are on course you will be increasing your value and the value of others. If you are off course, what are you willing to give up to get on course?

Formerly, I was a banker. The bank makes lots of money off you even if you have a free account. Know your banker by name and meet everyone in your branch from manager on down to the tellers. Give everyone your business card. When they hire a new manger, meet him/her right away. If they don't remember who you are when you come in, get a new bank. Seriously, if they don't care about you, they don't care about your money. Honor your value and worth. They might even give you an art show in the lobby. Do business with people you know and care about in your community.

If you're broke or struggling then ask yourself, "Do I spend more than I earn?" You have to either work harder, find ways to make more money or stop spending. Stop going out to eat! Eat well and prepare meals that YOU make at home.

Invest in your artist education. Experiment with your art at home if money is tight. No more five dollar lattes everyday on the way to work. Purchase books on prosperity, financial investing, inspiration, mind and body. to read and work with.

Let's face it getting to the Big Picture in the Artist's Business Life takes work. There is inspiration, vision, giving of your time and talent, doing the footwork and on-going action.

Alternatively, doing nothing leads to being broke and that is enough to kill your career. The good thing is that you can fix being broke but you can't fix being poor-minded. So, easiest way to enjoy that work is to enrich your mind. When you do this you find creative ways to stop being broke because the business of art is an art itself and broke just doesn't work in the business world! Your art business is a magical combination of many things and one that you have to shower with love, honor and value.

Stop taking a prospective customer to lunch or dinner just to show off and please a big ego. If you don't have the cash to do it, it can wait. You can also lower the ego's big shot standards and take a client or prospect out for a coffee. A very wealthy prospect of mine said to me once, "You know, I like to go for a slice of pizza or a hot dog and soda just as much as anybody else does." We became good friends over a relaxed slice of pizza; in fact it's those fun, simple things people tend to remember more than a fancy meal.

Bills, Bills, Bills

When you have bills, pay them! Take action now. Do you need to ask for advice about getting out of debt? I will tell you how to do it. PAY YOUR BILLS. The minute a bill arrives pay it, stop gambling on the due date. Always treat your creditors with respect; they didn't make your bills, you did. The highest interest rate debts get paid first. The lowest interest rates get minimum payments until the highest ones are gone. Then, start chunking down the next and the next. Pay on time all the time and don't blame your creditors for your bills; they stuck their neck out for you and gave you credit in the first place based on your promise to pay them back. Only use your credit for a business investment that is going to pay you a return. If you're not sure what that means then don't use your credit card. It takes a long time to pay down maxed-out credit. Be patient; don't be disillusioned. Credit card statements now show how long it takes to pay off your debt and most of your repayment goes to interest first. When paying bills such as credit cards, 1. Be grateful that somebody extended you their money to use and, 2. That you're actually putting your money in the bank when you pay them back! Make an affirmation, "I am putting money in the bank! That's right; you're putting your money in the bank. Tell yourself this when you pay your credit card bills. Act like you are writing yourself a check. Why? Because the Universe will respond no matter if you're putting your money in the bank to pay a bill or to save. Be grateful and creative and say, "Thank You! I am Putting Money in the Bank!"

Do you have a free checking account? If not, why? Do you have a cell phone plan that is padded with expense? Do you really need web access? Are you planning an intergalactic trip in the future? There are so many extra fees on things that it's ridiculous.

If you're in debt up to your eyeballs, make a list of stuff you could sell right now and then do it. Do you know what's in boxes that are packed away for over six months? This hoarded stuff is of no use to you any longer, so get it out and the energy moving. In my gallery, if things are in the storage room they may be necessary but must be non-income-producing items. Those unneeded storage items could yield a wealth of opportunity and benefit other folks. Out of sight art, is out of mind business and soon forgotten. Mind your business, overhead costs you!

Find creative, ethical ways to bring in multiple sources of income so you never have to get in a pinch again. Spend money only on necessities: Nutritious food made at home, shelter – mortgage, rent, utilities-electricity, water, gas (cable television, cell phone, is not a utility) and bills you need to pay back Get out of debt! Pay your bills! NO more starving artist!

Keep a small journal of everything you spend for the next three months and see where the money goes. For example, if you spend $3.95 per day at your local coffee house, that equals $1,441dollars a year. Now, add tax to that, the gas you spent driving there, the time you spent dilly-dallying and it starts getting expensive.

Creative Activity Points

Invest in good record keeping software and use it.

When you spend all the money budgeted for the month, stop spending and start selling more.

To keep things in perspective, start small. Make smart action plans with goals and a budget with manageable daily strategies and steps that are comfortable for you.

Set realistic pricing. You can always raise your prices. Never lower them; this upsets collectors and clients who are investing in your work.

Do not show art that you have no desire to sell or part with. If you must exhibit, get paid for loaning it. Rent it.

Study the Law of Compensation. Do a Google search on it and read up.

Make a list of things you could sell right now (such as odds and ends and things in storage). Then, sell them!

Do you know how much money you earn and how much money you owe?

Figure it out.

Draw yourself a symbol of what prosperity is to you. It does not need to be a material possession.

Get a free checking account.

Get a simple cell phone plan with unlimited minutes.

Pay your taxes first. If you are paying taxes, it means you're making money and you're thriving. Taxes are one of those things you have to take care of.

Be impeccable with your record keeping. Know your costs, keep every single receipt and hire an accountant for your taxes.

Shop around for insurance yearly. Rates on auto, home and apartment are competitive and you may get a better deal from a different agency even within the same company.

Be sure all your bank accounts are free of service charges.

Get a debit card that earns points in cash each time you use it. You'll be surprised how fast it adds up.

If you're bad with a credit card you may get in trouble with a debit card too. Always carry cash and once it's gone, go home.

Read books on being financially independent, developing a business and self-help. They can all change your prosperity consciousness.

Keep your receipts of what goes out (debits) and what comes in (credits) organized and separated by month.

Create different types of art to open up your creative channels and have fun.

When you create art and sell it, remember that you add to the economy.

Do not use credit cards to take prospective clients out to lunch or dinner.

Being a big shot with your credit brings big shot-sized bills to your doorstep.

Never assume someone won't appreciate your kindness or the simple things in life.

Make money, not excuses.

Tithe 10 percent of your gross income to someone or something that inspires you on an ongoing basis.

Take care of yourself and family first. Charity begins at home.

CHAPTER ELEVEN

Knowing What Other People Want The Art of Hearing and Listening

"I expect to pass through life but once. If therefore, there be any kindness I can show, or any good thing I can do to any fellow being, let me do it now, and not defer or neglect it, as I shall not pass this way again." —William Penn

What does knowing what other people want establish? The answer is an open door for you to bring your talents to market. What does the art of hearing and listening establish? The answer is your system of doing business.

Success is as simple as finding people to talk to, listening to their problems and then solving their problems by selling them your services and products. Tell people what you are doing. People want your stuff; however, they have to know what you're offering, where it is and how they can get it. Don't wait to be discovered! Discover yourself first and start letting people know about your find! You're an artist and you were born to contribute and share your gifts with the world.

When people found out that I was an artist they started asking for products and sometimes it was the same thing over and over again. Things like, "Can you paint a picture of my house or my pet?" or "Do you have your art on a T-shirt or a coffee mug? How can I get one?" Sometimes they just want an interesting story that goes with your art. They want to be able to treasure you and have a nice story that goes with it. So keep the story simple and good, not gossipy or the local dirt.

People love celebrity gossip and artists can be celebrities no matter the size of their career. You want them to remember your art style and your style of business! I suggest you leave the home life at home, the neighborhood dirt in the street and celebrate the business success in public. People want your product.

Do your research and find out if they want what you have to offer. They may not want the product you currently have. Don't take it personally. It's not about you! Take your work seriously, not yourself! And be kind. There are lots of fabulous products that have no audiences, customers or homes. Find out what your customers want, then create the product for them with your art on it! Take notes and create your system through the art of listening.

3 Things People Want to Know

There are three things people want to know about your business and service or product, although they may ask for it differently.

1. What is it that will help me with my problem? (I need pictures on my walls.)

2. How fast can I get it? (I'd like to take the art home right now.)

3. How much will this art cost me? (Even though you don't know it, I'm prepared to buy the art.)

Always put yourself in the shoes of your customer. Does this sound familiar? Have you asked these questions yourself about services or products at other people's businesses? Ask quality, empowering questions of others and listen intently to their answers.

How do you tell people about your business, service, or products then get them to it? Through social media, blogs, email, flyovers, billboards, postcards, video, word of mouth, webinar, speaking engagement, workshop, storefront? There are many ways to tell your story but nothing works like a live face-to-face meeting with a client or customer.

How do you tell others about your art? Word of mouth? If so, who do you tell? Everyone?

Start collecting e-mail addresses. What do you do with them? You have to use them or they serve no purpose.

Throw a party to introduce your art. Who do you invite? Do you have to host it or can you have someone sponsor you? Can you team up with another artist or business that works well with your product?

Think about The Big Picture. Do all these ideas fit in?

Do you have a product or service? Are you looking for new business success?

As a customer, yourself what do you want? Chances are good that others want it as well. Can you fill a need?

Set a goal and get on it. Keep track of what works and write it down in a systems journal. A systems journal is a record of what works in your art business. It is an owners guide or procedure manual that you follow for success. A system is what makes a business valuable. My system book was a big part of writing this book for you. By keeping track what worked for me I can now share with you.

Create a website and be sure you can collect vital customer info on the website such as email addresses for newsletters and correspondence so they can hear from you regarding new art and interesting things you may want to share back with them. How do you get customers to your web pages? They have to know who you are and what you have. E-mail them; message them via social media or video message them. A portfolio is not enough. A website just sitting there is not enough.

Write a press release that is newsy and tells people what you are doing, what you made and that it is available, how it benefits them and the community. If you want it to be in the news it must be newsworthy. Make a video and do the same thing in the film clip. Where do you post it? Same places, different places, everywhere you can? Be creative.

Creative Activity Points

Always have and carry your business card with you.

Collect pertinent, practical and useful information to identify where your market lies. Use common sense in marketing and do research. If you are an artist who paints pictures you probably would NOT want to market to other artists who paint pictures, unless you believe they are going to buy your art. You want to market to people who buy pictures from artists who paint pictures. Because of not doing homework some entrepreneurs spend a fortune advertising and setting up shop in the wrong places. The hip urban neighborhood with cool buildings and trendy restaurant might appear to be great but if the folks going there only do so between 9.pm and 11 p.m. for cocktails you must cater to that audience. Who and where are you customers? Where do they hang out? Do business there; that's where your sale is. Once you discover the customer ask questions about what they like and listen intently to the answers.

Many times the people that irritate you the most teach you valuable lessons. Value the wisdom of others while following your heart.

Present your artwork and yourself as a professional. Your viewers should respect you and your art before they ever see you or the art.

People will always ask why you make the art you do. They want to know. Have short and precise quality answers ready. They want to know things like this: "What inspired you to make this art piece of the flowers?" a good answer would be, "It was a glorious day, I was so happy and I ran home right away and capture the feeling, this is my tribute to that moment." The let them talk so you can learn more about your customer. Memorize your artist statement, story and biography.

Read publications such as: The Wall Street Journal, Inc. Magazine, Business Week, Entrepreneur, Fortune, and Forbes and don't laugh when you read an article on the millionaire artist. However, do take notes.

What makes art salable is its descriptive strength and perceived value of the artist behind it.

Never apologize for flaws in your art or your life, describe only the best aspects of your creations with accuracy.

Leave your home life at home and celebrate business success publicly.

Be clear on your expectations, as well as clearly understand the expectations of your clients. What does everybody want?

Sign up with affiliate programs that you find helpful and having integrity. If it sounds too good to be true, well, you know the rest.

Sell other persons products you believe in through their affiliate programs and create passive income.

BALBOA PARK

STUDIO FOUR

Harmony and Care

Step Four: Build Interpersonal Growth.

Studio Four covers Taking Care of Yourself and Your Body
- Tending to your Relationships - Nurturing Healthy Connections
Releasing Unhealthy Relationships
Laughing at Your Ego - Surrounding Yourself with Love, and Support

CHAPTER TWELVE

Nurture your Spirit by Clearing your Clouded Mind

"Three rules of work: Out of clutter find simplicity; from discord find harmony; In the middle of difficulty lies opportunity." —Albert Einstein

Start the day right off the bat with some quiet "me" time even if you have to get up early. This is important. Set your clock one hour earlier than everyone else in the house if necessary. Think about the things you really want to attract in your life, your dreams and desires. I meditate in quiet first; then I visualize. Let's talk about meditation first.

Remember Your Artist Spirit

Artists are image-makers. Be that artist. Imagine in your mind who you want to be. Let it go and now be that person you want to be. Act as if you are already that person. Dress, walk, talk and behave as if you are already that person. Why? Because You ARE that person. When you build the image in your mind and turn it over to the power within, Spirit, God force, the universal powers that be, your image moves into form. Be quiet and get in touch with your Artist Spirit. Be still and let your ideas gel. Meditate on it; there are many books on meditation and different ways to do it. Most everyone I know who meditates on a regular basis says the same thing: sit and be quiet with yourself. Focus on your breathing, in and out, and be quiet, Thoughts will come and go, which by the way is natural. Just focus on your breathing and the air going in and out of your body. At first it might be awkward to do this for even five minutes. However, after a while, you will begin to enjoy it and look forward to your quiet time of meditation. It's a stress reliever too, so it's actually good for you!

Meditation

Meditation is different from prayer. Prayer is asking; meditation is listening. You'll have to make quiet time for yourself in order to meditate. Like prayer, you can do it anywhere or anytime. Be patient and learn to meditate. Even five minutes is enough time; you can use a little more time to visualize after meditation. The more you do this, the more you will create easier accessibility to your subconscious mind. Take time to think out critical issues and listen for the answers. Most of the time answers do not come instantly. Be patient.

Make time to get quiet. Start small (say five minutes) and then work up to 30, 60 and 90-minute uninterrupted time periods. You may find that ten to fifteen minutes once a day is plenty When you have quiet time, you activate your super subconscious and trigger intuition, your inner genius. In your quiet time you can also go for a walk, do a chore and move about in quiet structure. However, I like to sit and be quiet for at least five minutes in the morning and five minutes in the evening.

It is important to relax, replenish and get grounded. Take time to find the natural rhythms of your body and rejuvenate your emotions, energy and vitality. This assists in taking that fuzzy little picture of what you want all the way to a clear Big Picture.

Here's one of my quick little meditations. If you're not sure how to meditate, try this one during the quiet time you've created for yourself in the morning or the evening.

The Artist Meditation:

1. Sit quietly and straight up in a firm but comfortable chair with both my feet on the ground.
2. Begin to pay attention to your breathing. Breathe in deeply and breathe out deeply, and as you do this you will begin to relax your body. Try it. Breathe in and breathe out, breathe in and breathe out.
3. Then, begin to relax. Start with your toes. Relax your toes completely; breathe in breathe out. Now, relax your feet; breathe in and breathe out. Your toes and your feet are both relaxed. Breathe in and breathe out. Now, relax your ankles, your lower legs, your upper legs, your hips, your buttocks, your abdomen, your chest area and your shoulders. Breathe in and out; relax your arms, wrists and hands. Breathe in; breathe out. Relax your neck, your jaw, your facial muscles; breathe in; breathe out. You will notice that your breathing has become lighter as you relax your body.

Do this for a full five minutes. Just concentrate on relaxing your body and breathing. As you become more comfortable meditating, you can drift off and dream and let the thoughts come and go, taking yourself to lovely places of rest and relaxation where sometimes brilliant ideas come to you.

One thing I like to do during meditation is picture myself in a beautiful sunny meadow sitting or laying on the beautiful grass and enjoying the peaceful setting. When I am ready I come back to the room fully where I'm sitting and then do some visualization exercises, which we will get to in a bit.

If you fall asleep, don't worry; your body may need to rest.

Your body is a magnificent vehicle that houses your soul and artist spirit; treat it well and it will carry you to amazing places. By doing daily meditation, you value and honor your body and appreciate its worth. Spirit provides you with access to endless resources. Quiet meditation sparks the creativity you seek.

The secret to your Big Picture is whispering in your ear. Each person has his or her own unique story. Only you can share yours.

There are common basics to success available but most importantly, follow your heart and your hunches. Get quiet everyday and listen for the whispers. You'll receive them easier through meditation. *Are you listening?*

Other Meditation Exercises:

Go for a quiet walk every day and let your body go for 30 to 60 minutes. Physical, quiet exercise is one of the best forms of meditation. Often after quiet exercising, you may gain insight and unexpected new creative ideas. This works for me and I hope it works for you too. Getting outside is also a form of getting grounded.

Literally get grounded; take off your shoes and socks and stand on the earth and imagine sending all your stressful energy into the ground where it can be released and recycled. If you can't do that, purchase a container or clay pot, some potting soil and some small plants or flowers. Get your hands in the dirt and create a little potted garden. This is wonderful quieting, grounding exercise.

Notice that these are quiet exercises, not noisy ones.

A physical work out is another form of meditation. However, be conscious of your environment. Many gyms have music blasting, people yelling and 24 hour news channels bombarding you with images of total negativity. Meditation affects your creative subconscious. Think twice about the places where you exercise.

Meditation exercises help you develop living-in-the-moment skills and powerful tools for nurturing your creative and grounding artistic spirit within.

Action Vs. Distraction

Let's talk about action versus distraction. Before you sign up for a year long course on spirituality, meditation or getting in touch with your higher spirit self, consider the art of distraction. As I mentioned earlier in the chapter, the best way to do this is to be quiet everyday for a short period of time. All the high integrity spiritual leaders tell you this. Beware of persons who intellectualize spirituality for profit. Do you really need to pay for a yearlong course to find out that all you need to do is sit and be quiet with yourself in order to tap into spirit? Or, is this your way of procrastinating and being distracted?

Meditate and Appreciate!

Now, to some of you, meditation may seem pretty dull. Everything you desire to have as an artist really has two sides to it. What you want in order to make a living and what you don't have. Where you place your focus regarding your heart's desire (intention) will bring it in either quicker or slower. It all comes down to how your desire feels inside to you.

What you want (or the absence of what you want) regarding making a living with your art all depends upon you. If thinking about your art career feels good, great! But if you then start thinking about why you don't have the art career you want, then you have to stop. Take a breather. Get back on track. This activates your magnetism and helps you get precisely what you want.

This is why it's so important to appreciate things around you. Then, allow your desires to come to you. Appreciation is fun thinking; meditation is quiet thinking. If meditation is difficult for you, learn to appreciate things around you. What you want will be attracted to you just the same but in a more fun-filled, exciting way. Use the same amount of time in the day, say fifteen minutes, to appreciate everything around you.

Chapter Twelve's Studio Play Sheet

Don't distort your Big Picture. Stop talking about the past and stay focused on the present moment while you think forward into the future. Think in a manner that says that things you have created and accomplished are now real. Avoid conversations of future tragedy; that is unreal and a waste of time and life. If there is a real tragedy tugging on your heart, find ways to resolve it or shut up about it. Nurture the bright essence of your artist spirit. To keep your artist spirit bright, put yourself only in situations that are supportive and caring. Be open to receive from sources that nourish your emotional wellness.

Pay attention to what you worry about from one day to the next. Take a small notebook and write down what you would rather focus on.

Take time by yourself today and everyday to rest, relax, breathe slowly and replenish. Take your time eating your meals at a gentle pace.

Get outdoors more often. Go for a brisk walk by yourself and into nature when possible and at your halfway point, slow down and relax the rest of the way. Enjoy breathing the air and noticing how many beautiful things there are. When possible, sit in a quiet place undisturbed for at least fifteen minutes. Stop and notice something outside yourself. Smell the flowers, feel the brisk air and observe the weather.

Park a block or two away from work and walk a little farther to your office or place of business. While outdoors, notice something to appreciate outside of yourself and say out-loud, "Wow!" or "My goodness, that's great!" Do this every day! Try it once an hour. Do it while driving in your car, walking, or just resting in place. Appreciate something you had nothing to do with creating. Do this for five minutes without interruption and see how it makes you feel inside!

Be gentle and kind to yourself and others. Enjoy meeting with people and being in the moment. Keep the topic of your conversations to the wonderful things going on in the present, omitting the past and the future.

Focus on your "can do's" and feel how they make you and everyone around you happier because you are thinking and doing what you love to do. Allow yourself to daydream bigger. Ask yourself- *What was it that I did that brought this about?* Then come back after your walk or quiet time and get out your notebook.

Did you have any insights or new ideas? They may have something to do with your dream list or not. You may have an "AH HA" moment that is entirely different or unrelated to your business. Did you write them down, drawing the lines on blank paper or sticky notes? This is your inner guidance, inspiration and brilliance coming through. Do this a little bit everyday and learn to focus more on things you appreciate. Remember the blank check from the Universe mentioned earlier? It's calling you through the Big Picture you are creating for yourself, the one you might later share with others.

Ask your creator, higher power, source or the Universe for need guidance in staying focused.

Write down all the details of your issues and problems. Write new ideas and solutions, no matter how outlandish. Get those ideas out of your head and onto the paper. Sometimes, as you focus quietly, you can solve an issue at hand this way.

Get a book or e-book on daily meditation at the local bookstore, web store, or library. Find a book that resonates with you. There are many meditation books available.

Practice a daily quiet meditation of some sort for at least five to fifteen minutes in the morning and five to fifteen minutes in the evening. Get into this new habit.

Think about and reflect upon your life experience. This builds wisdom, insight and helps you make better decisions.

Just as an artist does with creating a portfolio, you can build the image of your Big Picture with a series of small pictures that is a collection but this one is in your mind in your mind. See yourself the way you want to be. Do this by starting where you want to end up. Do this by remembering the future with a grand finale, the end of the movie, book, etc. and remember to include the vision of your art business success in it too! Make a written description in the present tense about your future. Do it right now.

As an artist, be a picture maker. Create an image of how you want to be deep inside your mind. Let go and be that person you want to be. When you build the image and turn it over to the power within, you are letting Spirit lead. You are letting go and letting God. If the word 'God' offends you, use another powerful word for that energy that drives the Universe and everything in it. Go to the God/Spirit word within you, the ever-present energy in all and turn it over to that Spirit. Spirit will move your image into the form. Be quiet, get in touch and look within. People get the phrase, 'letting go and letting God' confused with religious ceremony. I'm not talking about a religious experience at all, so please don't misunderstand this concept.

The power of ever-present energy is in all things and within you too. It's an omnipresent energy force, which you don't have to believe exists because it is there, nonetheless, right down to sub-atomic particles.

Everything manmade thing around us in our human environment was first a thought. Someone had an idea that caused the manmade thing you enjoy to be transformed from thought into form somewhere along the way. Science backs up this, too. Intuition is sort of like going fishing in the Universe; you cast your line and believe you will snag an answer. We wait for subtle answers in meditation. Be patient and let the answer come to you. At the right time, the energy of your feelings catches up and syncs with what you desire. So let it.

Once you create and make your art available for sale, become responsible to yourself, your financial destiny and your heirs. Don't wait to protect your artist rights. Protect your ideas; investigate copyrights and trademarks. Yes, you need to copyright your work in business. It's not expensive when you do it correctly. Save yourself a ton of time and headaches. Consult with an attorney who deals in intellectual property copyrights. Consult the copyright office. Their job is to answer your questions; they get paid to do that. Consultations are usually free.

As you develop your business system, make reasonable efforts to keep your trade secrets confidential and share them on a need-to-know basis. This does not mean being mysterious; this means being honorable to you. Blabbing to everyone down at the coffee shop about your newfound gold mine house is not a very smart way of securing your future fortune nor is being so reclusive about your art that no person ever gets to see your brilliance either. Having a confidentiality agreement in place might be a good idea for people who work with you and for you.

When you are employed to create art for someone else (or a business entity), the art belongs to them. Creating for them is part of your job. So you can see that it's a good idea to be an entrepreneur. License your art work and earn income while keeping the rights to it.

Creative Activity Points

An overworked mind and body equals no business. Take care of your body and mind; when you do it takes care of you. Invest in personal quiet time.

Connect with nature and do something physical each day. This opens you up to new ideas.

Selling original art is not the only way to make money with your art career. Investigate all sorts of art reproduction avenues.

Copyright your art creations through the government copyright office and not through systems of urban legend and hearsay. The most common and misleading piece of advice I always hear is: To protect art from copyright infringement before you publish your art mail an unopened postmarked package containing and image of the art to yourself. Do not open it, keep it sealed always. If you ever have to go to court you bring the unopened mail with your for proof. I have even heard this one from art professors! This is NOT true, don't do it. The way you copyright your work is through the copyright office…period.

Keep and respect confidentiality in your business and businesses belonging to others, as well.

Have confidentiality agreements in place with people who work with you and for you.

Investigate trademarks and protect your brand.

Licensing your art is a great source of additional income.

Appreciate your progress right now.

CHAPTER THIRTEEN

Magnetize What You Want

*"We can only be said to be alive in those moments when our
hearts are conscious of our treasures."* —Thornton Wilder

It's hard to imagine any type of artistic success when your finances are out of control. Successes and failures aren't caused by money. Money is just a thing; basically it's paper with ink on it. Money can be made of metal and even made of plastic in some countries. It is used as an exchange of appreciation and energy. In this world, money is a trade tool, which allows you to experience things you love in life. So, what is your relationship with money in the first place? How can you understand yourself better with regard to money? You can tell pretty fast how you feel about it; if you do not have enough of it, you might feel pretty lousy. Until you learn to respect and appreciate money, no amount will ever be enough. Money represents energy; perhaps it's no shocker that it's called it 'currency.'

Everything, including money, is made from energy. Energy is a truly indestructible force. It never dies or diminishes; it merely transmutes form through rates of vibration and mediums. Physical objects that appear solid are actually not. We are all made up of the same thing (energy) and what separates us is the vibration, the energy. The more stable a vibration, the more solid the object appears. The opposite is true; the less stable, the less solid. Now, this will mess with your head-what separates all form is…nothing! Nothing physical separates you from any other form. The energy that makes up you and I has always been and always shall be present.

Everything that is going on in your life is a mere example of how your energy flows through those experiences. Health, relationships, and money are just another reflection in the mirror and one that is full of useful information. These reflections tell us what is going on in our consciousness; in other words, what is working and what is not. You may be working yourself to death and have no money or hardly working and have much money. No matter what your income, you can develop and experience prosperity and success.

My friend, artist Bonnie Druschel, says, "The more I love myself and treat myself with kindness, the more my life just keeps getting better and better." Gratitude and love are great multipliers for magnetizing money and causing money to stick around. When you feel good and send out goodness and gratitude, rewards come back to you. Do people who have the most amount of money complain the most about it? Usually not. So who does? Have you noticed how people who provide the minimum service required at work seem to continually complain about wages and under appreciation? The employees providing added value get promoted and zoom up and out to better places. It's often heard in the workplace, "the good ones never stay." Well they don't have to stay; gratitude called them to higher service, which benefited them monetarily.

When you decide to make a living as an artist, money is going to be involved. What is your relationship with money, just you and money? Most people have difficulty here. Sit and be quiet for about five to seven minutes and ponder these questions:

Do you respect money?
Are you scared of money?
Are you superstitious about money?
Are you grateful for money?
Do you see money as a tool to do great things?
Do you repel or magnetize money?
Are you a starving artist or a thriving artist?
Do you just get by at work to keep your job?
Do you just get by every month financially?
Do you even know how much money you have?
What is your actual worth?

Could you feel thankful for the money, sale, new or returning customer or the commission even before it has arrived? Could you feel grateful even if it never showed up at all?

You become successful by honoring and valuing your time and worth. It is imperative that you know your monetary worth and value. (Most computers come with built-in money programs.) Make a list of your assets and liabilities, take a look around your home, add up the value, (your income), then add up your overhead, (your liabilities). You have to know what your liabilities and worth are in order to know what you must earn to cover your expenses. Think about this seriously. If you require $12 an hour to get by and you are making $10 an hour in wages, it won't be long before you are upside monetarily and in trouble financially. By knowing your value and worth, you are honoring yourself. This aids you in getting on the road to abundance and the sooner the better!

If you can envision and create an art piece why not do the same with your own prosperity? Of course, you can! You are a money mirror and a magnet to money. Once again, everything is energy, including you and me. If you were sitting next to a stack of money on a nearby table and there was space between you and the money on the table, what would you call the space between you and that money? If you replied, "Nothing," you are correct. (By the way, this applies to just about everything that you desire.) What stands between you and the money or another person, place or thing is nothing. We are all connected by energy. So, then apply some energy in order to attract and magnetize the things you appreciate.

What's Your Magnetism Setting?

Are you magnetized for disappointing or promising financial events? Many folks look for ways to cut back financially. While this is noble and sometimes necessary, it would be much better to think of ways to create more or extra income and focus on prosperity instead of lack. It's the force of love in your life directed toward what you do that moves the money to or away from you. Think of ways to provide more value through love and gratitude with your energy. Avoid the action of cutting back, which stops the flow of wealth. Wealth flows to those artists who absolutely love and give value to everyone. Artists who slash prices and complain about how bad things are have a different and starker reality. These artists are actually magnets for disappointment and repel money. Money is an odd creature; it sticks around and magnetizes when you give more value than you receive. Having a fire sale on your art will just set up consumers to always expect low rock bottom prices from you and keep your work from appreciating in value.

If money is just ink on paper, then why can't you rewire your mind to change the zeros in your mind to a much greater number ($500 or $5,000)? One day I decided to create a "new zero," or a new energy. I realized that money is appreciation energy and that getting close to zero that the end of every month was sending me into fear so I decided to change where my "zero" was. It took some stretching mentally however here is what I did. I changed my zero to a new number, that if I went below I considered overdrawn in my bank account. Instead of freaking out as your checking account gets closer to zero, why not visualize your new zero ($500 or $5,000)? Rewire your mind. You can do this. Then don't drop below your "new zero." You can even penalize yourself if you fall below your new zero. Perhaps you might hold yourself to making a contribution or donation to an organization or political campaign that you do not like. Try first with a new number you can handle, say $100, and work your way up to qualify for interest-bearing checking account at your bank. This has an added benefit too, instead of trying to cut back on needed expenses and feed more lack in life you can focus to create and generate more positive income flow!

Chapter Thirteen's Studio Play Sheet

Did you answer the questions in this chapter about you and money?
If not, do so now.
Do you know and honor your self-worth? Write down the ways you do.
What is your actual net worth? Get a pad and paper and write down all the things you own from property to paperclips and the worth of all your bank accounts. You may be worth far more than you give yourself credit for.
Keep your actual net worth accessible to you with ease. It should not be a mystery to you.
Do you make ends meet? Do you end right back where you started every payday or month? Write down three creative ways to create a little extra income each month for yourself. Be willing to do them and give yourself a clear deadline to start doing them.

1.

2.

3.

My monthly expenses are:_____ I require $_____ in addition for savings. I require an additional $_____ for fun such as entertainment. My new total monthly expenses are now. $_____

Disappointment will happen. Deal with it and move on with optimism and promise of a better thing to come.
No longer accept unacceptable behavior such as worrying as your reward.
Volunteer at your favorite charity one hour a week and increase hours up from there.
Could you create your own charitable organization to help your community?
Investigate ways to have a little extra money for savings and fun? Write them down.
Envision and believe in your financial prosperity. Write down affirmative statements and start reading them daily.

CHANGE YOUR ZERO TO A NEW PLUS NUMBER.

Pay bills from a place of gratitude.
Feel thankfulness for the credit worthiness that has been granted to you.
Give to others from a place of prosperity and gratitude.

The $5,000.00 Game

What good could you do for others with $5,000? What if you woke up and there was a gift of this amount in your bank account? Would you go out and spend it? Then, what if the next day you woke up and there was another $5,000 deposited in your bank account? What if that happened every day for the rest of your life? What if that amount placed in your bank account doubled every day? $5, $10, $20, $40, $80, $160,000, and so on. Cool, huh?! There's a hitch though; you have to spend the money every day or you won't continue to receive it and you can only spend it if you are feeling grateful, loving thoughts of appreciation.

The Universe doesn't know if you really have it or not. However, the energy of feeling like you do will create prosperous feelings inside you that magnetizes wealth to you. Start noticing all the good stuff already around you because that is what kick-starts the Law of Attraction.

Spend five minutes right now thinking of all the things you could do with this money. Then, every day for the next thirty days, spend your $5000+ game money but never on the same thing twice. It's not as easy as you think.

Carry cash on a positive note. Be happy and grateful about when it's there!

Sort and carry your money bills face up, think of that side of it as positive and the other side as negative. As you use your money, send out feelings of love and appreciation with it, knowing that spending it betters someone else's life, as well as yours.

Appreciate your investors – gratefully pay bills back.

Think of the bills you receive as checks in the mail. You have been entrusted with responsibility because you are trustworthy. Write 'thank you' for the loan of trust you have been given on the payment stub. Think of all the people involved who made your loan, your credit, your car, your water, your electricity, your telephone and other things possible. Send back gratitude with your payment check, each and every time you pay a bill. You must feel gratitude in order to receive more of what you want. If you don't feel grateful, the energy you send out will bring you more debt. Be authentic when you do any exercise like this. Come from a place of love and thankfulness and then watch what happens! Whatever you are feeling inside is what you will magnetize more of.

Feeling really good about other people's monetary success, as well as your own, causes money to stick around no matter who is having the success. Feel really good and grateful for the success of others as it magnetizes all sorts of wealth and well being to you. There is a caveat here though; when you give from place of ego and needing to be a big shot, the Law of Attraction is going to kick in and bring you more lack. Do not be reckless here; be sincere and give from a true feeling of love, gratitude, value and honor. Better others with your sincere gifting.

Want to learn from true sales specialists? Kids and animals are great experts. Watch closely; they rarely struggle for what they want; they just ask for it until they get it. While there may be the occasional tantrum if they don't get what they want; it's no big deal. They simply drop it and move on to something else, releasing that request (demand). In the long run, they usually get what they desire or something even better. Observe those children or pets when they want something. How do they get what they want? Could you let go of the artist's struggle and the tantrums? Whether it's personal or business, could you let go of a relationship that just walked away? Could you let go of the judgment and the hate for someone who has 'done you wrong?' Could you just 'be' and anticipate expanding your art career with excitement and joyfulness without hanging onto the past? Lighten up, trust and believe and let the Law of Attraction bring the things you want to magnetize into your art career.

Creative Activity Points

Financial success carries through to your customers and non-customers as well; they want to be part of your success. Financial success grows from various ways besides the monetary. A good word on the street is future money in your pocket and in the bank.

A positive cash flow is a positive energy flow that people intuitively pick up on and energetically tap into; they want to contribute.

People may love a good drama in the movies but they love a good success story in the real world. Include your viewers into your success story with gratitude.

Spend less than you earn. Make more than you spend.

Strike a healthy balance. Invest in multiple sources of art income-generation. Save for fun memories of tomorrow.

The only discounts that you should offer are on purchases of very expensive original pieces of art that are paid for in installments. For example: three equal payments spread over a three-month period (the art is never delivered to the purchaser until fully paid for). However, if the payments are made early, you may give a discount off the full final payment. A two-percent discount is appropriate off the full price of the artwork.

Serve your customers with extra value (more love and gratitude) rather than discounts and fire sales. Offer free incentives (such as free shipping or free framing) instead of discounts in order to attract and magnetize a better clientele. Watch your give-away costs. Don't be foolish.

When you sincerely give more value, your art sales, business and art career will take off. When you give from a place of need and lack, you'll soon be broke, out of business and back on the poor farm complaining with the other starving artists.

Get your finances under control. Respect yours - and others - money. You can't make a living at anything until you learn to do this.

Observe how experts get their sale. Learn how to ask for the sale.

Learn how to let a sale go in the right way and at the right time.

Lighten up, trust, believe and love magnetizing the very things you want.

CHAPTER FOUTEEN

Having Fun with Having Fun
Co-create a Future with Others!

"It's kind of fun to do the impossible." —Walt Disney

Are we having fun yet? You've got to get in the game. You should have your Big Picture goal(s) set. If you don't, what are you waiting for? Another book or workshop you need to attend? Come on people, let's get rolling; perhaps some fun is what you need. Get your game on. To some people the number seven is lucky. So let's use the number seven in this situation. How would you like to achieve your seven-year goals in seven months or less?

My friend Kathleen Reinhardt threw a party and she learned and shared this technique from Jack Canfield's book,"The Success Principles." We both now use this game and throw a Come as You Are party about once a year for friends and associates. I highly recommend Jack's book and suggest studying it from cover to cover. Okay, back to the story. A few years ago, Kathleen invited me to her party. She informed me and other guests that it was a theme party and that we were to come as the person we wanted to be seven years from now, with props! And we were to remain in character the entire evening. *An interesting and exciting concept*, I thought to myself. *I needed new and challenging fun. I'm in! I am ready to arrive!*

We all created props and got dressed up. I had the time of my life and everyone really got into it! I ran into people I knew and people I didn't know. One of the guests came as Kathleen's personal chef and she actually catered the entire evening. As we ate delicious delicacies, we learned that our illustrious chef traveled the planet preparing gourmet meals for the world's elite. Tonight it would be our turn to feast. We stayed in character all evening, taking ownership of our success, talking about our achievements and shared what we were doing with our lives. I went as a successful gallery owner who was known as the California Artist and told the story of how I spoke at universities and wrote books about the way I accomplished all this. I brought two mock up magazine covers that I made on my computer, one of which was an interview written by Oprah Winfrey on my charitable art foundation. They appeared so authentic that a few folks thought they were real! It was a lot of fun. While I was there, I had a friend call me on my cell phone stating that it was the White House and the President would like me to come to Washington D.C. and give art lessons to the First Family. I had my friends phone number pre-programmed into my phone as "The White House" so when it rang I held up the incoming screen message in the phone to everybody and said "Oh my! It's the White House on the phone. LOOK! I'd better take this call!" The evening was a very powerful experience for everyone. I left the party energized and very encouraged. People who attended still talk about that night.

To make a long story short, in the time since Kathleen's party (only a few short years later) I opened my first little gallery inside the most visited state park in California. I represented my city and state with my paintings and became a best-selling author. While I have yet to be interviewed by Oprah or give art lessons at the White House, you'll see letters from the White House thanking me and other artists for our volunteer work in the arts if you come to visit my gallery in Old Town San Diego State Historic Park. You'll also notice an invitation to bring our pieces to the White House for display! Other folks who attended that evening have manifested owning a home, relationships, new businesses and fully paid-for dream vacations. Not bad for three hours of fun. We personally learned that night at Kathleen's that once you send a powerful message to your crew in your subconscious, you set the wheels of the Universe in motion and you just never know what can manifest. So, BE PRECISE! As a side note, in addition to your personal success, always be sure to include the success of your art business and that of your friends' businesses as well when playing any of these visualization games.

Chapter Fourteen's Studio Play Sheet

The Big Picture Party of Tomorrow

Reward yourself and throw a party like the Big Picture Party. This exercise is fun, very powerful and has manifested amazing realities.

Seven weeks from now you are going to throw a party. It is going to be a theme party. At this party, you are living your ideal life. Remember, you are living seven years into the future from today. Let me ask you this. If you had unlimited resources and could do anything you wanted who would you be, what would you do, and what would you have? How does that make you feel inside just knowing that anything is possible?

Who do you really want to become? Write it down and share it with seven different people today as if you are already that person. Insert an invitation something like this:

> ### You're Invited
>
> Imagine that seven years from today you would be living your ideal life. The Big Picture. You have all that you need and you are financially independent, happy healthy, in great shape and living the life of your dreams. What are you doing? What have you accomplished? Who are you exactly? We'd like to know.
>
> Come to this party and tell us all about it.
>
> Are you a world-famous author, artist or entrepreneur? Are you retired and living the life of your dreams on a secluded beach? Are you married or single? Are you traveling the world first-class? Do you have your own TV show? Did you move to the city, country, perhaps an exotic island? Did you win the lottery? What have you been up to these last seven years into the future? Everyone at the party would like to know.
>
> Please bring props to show us what you have accomplished.
>
> Please be prepared to spend two to three hours of your evening mingling, laughing, and making new friends and seeing old friends who just happen to be some of the most successful and inspiring persons you've ever met.

At The Big Picture party you will be in character for the entire event and you will be acting as if you are already that person. You have seven weeks to design fun props, and any other elements that would enhance the character you are going to portray. Please follow the directions enclosed to your magnificent party and show up as the person you are seven years from now.

You can tailor the party to however many people you feel comfortable. You could hire someone to photograph and film the event, then send mementos to everyone who attended. It's really up to you and the possibilities of fun are truly unlimited. Acting as if you have achieved your goals is not as important as what you become *inside* by acting out and feeling that you have achieved your goals.

As you were asked earlier in this book, have you done that thing you wanted to do five years ago? How about seven years ago? If not, why? Don't miss the party! Now's your chance to live out your dreams and have fun. What are you waiting for? If you don't take any action toward your dreams and goals today, what will you be doing five years from now? Still stuck in the same place?

If a large party is too overwhelming you can host a smaller intimate affair, like a lunch or dinner with two or three friends. What is important is that you celebrate your future Big Picture today! By participating in this game and talking to others who are not emotionally involved with your goals you will gain new perspectives and new ideas. This party can be truly life changing and could possibly magnetize your Big Picture to you faster than ever. Alert the Press! You're arriving!

Creative Activity Points

Be an ambassador and force for all that is good. Throw a party with no sales pitches attached. Loosen up, be friends and play.

When it's all said and done, it's family, friends and the fun that we've had that counts.

Send out a hand written note card to ten friends a week until you exhaust your friends' list, telling them how much you appreciate them. E-mails and texts don't count. The human touch is what's often missing in our lives. Be a real friend, not a text screen that's ignored or forgotten when the 'inbox' is full.

Sometimes you have to say "No" to the party, the dinner or the pot-luck. It's okay; it's good to say no, but not all the time.

Everyone needs quiet time to rest up and create.

Develop a success-based story about your art to share and always be able to refer to it should you be caught off guard by the real press.

Build a championship of team players in your business, including sales and marketing.

Everyone wants to win the game!

Talented people naturally want to work for great employers.

Customers prefer to purchase products and services from artists that tell the story of their strong co-creative culture.

Consider putting on a group art show for a good cause. There is a lot of power in collective co-creating, which brings healthy vision to the community.

Celebrate success in big ways or small ways; it doesn't matter the size of the party; what matters is that you celebrate it.

CHAPTER FIFTEEN

Take a Y.O.U. Turn

*"Setting an example is not the main means of influencing another;
It is the only means."* —Albert Einstein

GETTING BACK TO BASICS

Okay, it is a given that we are told that if we eat right and exercise, we will be happier and healthier. Yet most people don't follow this sage advice. After all, it takes discipline, doesn't it? Don't wait for health or tragedy to strike! Start taking caring of yourself right away; take baby steps so you don't become overwhelmed. Eat balanced meals and take care of your physical self so you can think clearly and have the energy to make a living with your art career.

The secret key to making more money, getting more art shows and living the life of your dreams is giving more positive, upbeat and enthusiastic art presentations. Feel a genuine belief inside yourself that you are already there and in possession of your end result.

This is not just in showing and selling your products; it applies to your whole life and how you present yourself to others. Just as in the previous chapter where you played the Come as You Are Party, life can reflect that exciting possibility every day.

TAKE CARE OF YOUR BODY

Your physical body is a manifestation of what's going on inside you, as well as what's happening externally with your relationships. Let's face it; there's nothing fun about feeling unhealthy and sick inside and out.

Learn how to create happy, healthy meals at home and when going out to dinner order healthy nutritious meals, as well. Most restaurants feature healthy items on their menus. With some practice you will know what's good for you and what's not. Whatever you are feeding your body is also feeding your mind. As with everything else we've discussed, see yourself where you want to be and take balanced action steps to get there.

Life can be a true masterpiece. However, if you come across negatively, after a while no one will want anything to do with you, no matter how popular you may become or how you sugarcoat your presentations,. You can always make more money but never more time. Make the most of your time by taking care of your magnificent body, since you only get one. Learn how to create a positive, upbeat and healthy life. Keep moving forward with it and everything else will follow.

The Power of Reflection

The more you focus on the good stuff, the less powerful and prevalent the bad stuff becomes. There is great power in either one. Which thing do you want to give the most power to? As you've heard before, it's your Big Picture and it is your responsibility.

Have you ever had an older person say to you, "If I knew what I know now when I was your age, I would've done things differently!" Let me ask you something similar. Is there something that you would not have done or been involved with again today if you knew then what you know now? Something like a relationship, organization, membership, investment, that box of jelly doughnuts or a job?

One of the biggest time wasters of all is pursuing a course of action, job, diet, or relationship that is not suited to you. Many people waste many of years working at something that they don't like, believe in, or enjoy. Can you relate to what I'm saying? Stress is the key indicator that something is not right. If you are unhappy in a situation and continue with it, then it is unlikely that the situation will change. Do you have the courage to change your thinking or situation? Or, are you stuck and becoming increasingly unhealthy and unhappy?

Balance, Balance and More Balance

Most everyone wants to live a happy, healthy and harmonious life. Much of our happiness comes from relationships we form on the job but we should be clear that keeping life in balance and being happy at home should be the number one priority. The main reason people go to work is to earn an income, which allows them to enjoy relationships, health and other important parts of personal life. Unfortunately, many of us put the cart before the horse and over do the work part to obtain more free time and "stuff" for the ones we love. What often happens is that we lose focus, wind up working all the time and stop putting our loved ones first. The people we care for the most begin to suffer.

Sometimes we even become resentful of the ones we love because of work stress. Either we are working too much or they are. We suffer and become guilty. Some persons seek distraction through destructive means in order to escape, turning to drugs, alcohol, sex, gossip and other reckless pursuits of escape. The fortunate few will figure out a better way to live. Some may seek a support group and/or professional help, such as therapy or counseling.

Who do you get professional advice from? Do they have integrity and follow their own advice and live accordingly? If your physician, life coach or spiritual advisor were overweight and smelled of cigarettes, would you take them seriously if they advised you on a weight loss or quit smoking program? If your best friend has their divorce attorney on speed dial or lives with an abusive spouse, would you accept marital advice from them? Seriously, use your common sense and look for integrity in your professional and personal relationships. No matter what, always seek persons of integrity when you look for advice. You could always tap your intuitive artist spirit to make an assessment of the situation. Ask you self, Is this professional advice is serving my best and highest interest? Often you will get your answer right then and there from an inner feeling nudge yes or no. If you feel nothing, don't worry, but if you are worried, that in itself is a big hint telling you something.

Self-Care Is Essential

Dedicate one hour to self care every day and apply the 20/20/20 Rule of balance; do some of the exercises we've covered.

20 minutes of Meditation (Focus on empowering questions and be open to snagging some wonderful answers.)

20 minutes of Visioning (Get your vision board out right after meditation.)

20 minutes of exercise (Go for a twenty-minute walk to start. It grounds you.)

Make this a priority and enjoy yourself every day. You are constantly building images in your mind. See yourself the way you want to be. Then, jump into that role and start playing it. Why wait? Banks have no problem raising their interest rates so why not raise your own interest rate in yourself?! Talk about increasing value in your artist spirit bank account!

Again, start where you want to end up. Do this by remembering your own future Big Picture.

Prepare a written description in the present tense of where you want to be. Make a life script for success. Be precise and positive, removing words such as 'want' or 'wish,' and replace them with words and phrases such as, 'I am' and 'I now____'. These are powerful statements that describe where you are in life.

Responding vs. Reacting

A word to the wise; some unwanted things and situations around, money, relationships, and old thought patterns may continue to pop up that you no longer want. DO NOT be discouraged! It takes a while to retrain the subconscious crew; they're used to the old method of doing things and old thought adventures you launched a while ago. So be aware and say, 'No thank you' and be patient as you move forward with your eye on The Big Picture. Think of it this way. It's like we are all at this big cocktail party that the Universe has thrown for us. It's a once-in-a-lifetime party and WOW! We get to go! We arrive expecting the very best of everything and the first tray of delicacies comes out for you to sample and…YUCK! You holler, "That's not what

I want to eat; I thought this was going to be scrumptious! I'm outta here!" You leave the party. Meanwhile, you could have said, "No thanks," because on the very next tray is exactly what you wanted or something better! You reacted instead of responding with patience, missed the boat and left the party stressed. Don't miss the boat. Stay with it and stay on course.

Free Will is Yours

The secret password to success is YOU. You have within you right now to be, do and have whatever you wish to create. Good, bad, indifferent, chaotic, peaceful, joyous, prosperous, lacking, abundant, fabulous health, you name it. Let's go to the artistic power within. We are all connected to that Artist Spirit through energy that permeates all things.

You have free will; everyone does. You have common sense and the ability to make choices. You have the ability to regenerate and start your day over at any given moment, and you also have the ability to follow through, make decisions, magnetize your desires and leave this place better than you found it, so do it! What choices are you willing to make to improve your success?

You are being set up! Yes that's true. Good, bad or indifferent, you are being set up and you are doing it to yourself. We all set ourselves up through our defining our expectations. So why not set yourself up to receive what you want? You have to expect abundance in order to receive abundance. Expectation is a mindset that created the Law of Attraction. Many folks expect the worst to happen and guess what? They usually get it. What if you expected the best to happen? What if the world was out to do you good today?

Few people expect a windfall of abundance. However, when you turn your desires over to your artist spirit and choose to let go and release attachments, you are much more likely to get it.
*Something you Want = A YES thought
*Don't want = A NO thought (don't even go there)
An Abundance of Good = YES
An Abundance of Bad = NO
Get it?
It's our own 'yes' and 'no' energies that we put out there and they both magnetize.

The good stuff is already there for you it's inside, not external. When you think that some "out there event" is going to cause you wealth you are setting yourself up to fail. The good and both are bad here. It's about what you resonate with inside that attracts you to what's out there. You only see what you're in harmony with. That is why it's so good to be grateful for the wealth you all ready have so you can resonate with the good that's all ready there. What are you in harmony with? That is what you see.

Chapter Fifteen's Studio Play Sheet

Write a one or two page letter to yourself from the future about all the cool stuff that happened to you on your journey. Don't forget to thank yourself now for that magnificent life.

Write another one or two page letter to the public about you and your life one hundred years from now and how you changed the world for better.

Start the letter with: "One hundred years ago there was a (woman or man) named_____. The world today is a better place because of this person and here is their story." Proceed from there and just let your imagination flow; this is your chance to shine. So dream big.

Did you have any new insights from the previous two exercises?

Did you have any new and unexpected developments that will create new goals?

Did you take time to enjoy yourself today? Did you spark any new interest?

Apply the 20/20/20 rule of self-care with Meditation, Visioning and Physical Exercise.

Write a script of your perfect life as if it is happening right now. Start the script with an account from the moment you wake up in the morning until the evening when you go to sleep. Describe precisely what you do, where you go, how you live, travel, with whom, your finances and the way you spend your time having fun in your personal and public life. It's your life; tell the story of how you want it to be!

What have you learned so far?

Stories sell! Tell happy memorable stories about your art in three to four sentences. I have a painting titled "Bicycles in A Row" Most folks who see it say there is something about the piece that makes them happy. Here's an example of a short story I tell about it: "Let me tell you what inspired me to paint the bicycles I love the summer Olympics and wanted to do a painting to commemorate that. So I went for a walk to contemplate what I might create. Walking by a neighborhood bicycle shop and saw all these different color bikes in a row and their wheels which immediately gave me a happy feeling and reminded me of the Olympic Rings in this painting that you now see.

Find peace through forgiveness, both for yourself and others.

You've learned to take ownership of your Big Picture and you can have fun with others doing it too.

Make decisions by focusing on the solutions.

You have a magical mind and you can train it to attract what you want. It will begin to attract more and more, like compound interest; whatever you invest or deposit comes back to you.

You learn to serve the world from your heart first by identifying with gratitude what you love and by showing appreciation and kindness.

You do make the world a better place through your thinking, associations and what you are in harmony with.

Find and live your passions, following your inspirations to make a contribution.

You can have fun and play games with yourself, others and the Universe.

You are responsible for your relationships and it's up to you to surround yourself with love and support. Do it now.

You can magnetize prosperity through adding value, showing gratitude and giving back with a loving, open heart.

You can play.

Creative Activity Points

Act as if you are the success you desire and put it out there; have fun with it!

The good you can do by yourself is small compared to what you can accomplish with a positive, goal-minded group. Link up with other like-minded folks to create new possibilities.

Play and have fun at work and home.

Write a script for the perfect business plan you desire.

Include friends and colleagues in your fun time.

It's okay to say NO and relax.

Create balance and harmony between work and play.

The solution to one problem often presents another problem. Don't be afraid to get in touch with your inner artist to find a way to tackle these challenges and watch your artist living grow tenfold.

Point Loma Light - San Diego California

STUDIO FIVE
Be Illuminated

Step Five: Be In Grace

"I believe that painting should come through the avenues of meditation rather than the canals of action." —Mark Tobey

CHAPTER SIXTEEN

Affirmation and Emotion Feeling

"Let's not forget that the little emotions are the great captains of our lives and we obey them without realizing it." —Vincent Van Gogh

You may not know it, but you were born to thrive and prosper. You may be thinking yes, but how? Or, you've got to be kidding! Well, I for one am convinced that you were born to thrive and I'm not the only one that believes this. Many times others can see our potential way before we can. However, like an unplanted seed, sheer potential does no one any good unless it is nurtured. It's important to move away from simply being a person with great potential and toward being a person of manifested purpose and service.

Breathe in the air; there is plenty for you. It is abundant evidence for you. Enjoy the daylight; it is also abundant evidence for you. Enjoy the evening; it too is abundant evidence for you. The natural abundance in nature, of which you are a part, is evidence that there is plenty for you and it is unconditional. There is more than enough air, there is more than enough sunshine, dirt, rocks, and on it goes. There is also more than enough money. There are more than enough venues for your art and more than enough ideas, customers, clients, walls, rooms, halls, spaces, riches and on it goes. Can you picture more places that await your artistry?

Seeing pictures and thinking thoughts can evoke emotions and feelings. As we reviewed earlier thinking of holding a loving puppy or kitten and the unconditional love feeling it evokes, creates strong feelings inside me. Does it do that for you?

Here's a fun exercise: Think of when holding a loving puppy or kitten and that warm and fuzzy feeling you get inside. Now, RELAX and transfer that same feeling into attracting the thing you want. If puppies or kitties don't do it for you, think of something loving that makes you melt and do the same thing.

We live in a natural Universe and a world of abundance. You can naturally develop a mentality of abundance. Do not allow the illusion of limited resources or scarcity of others to become part of who you are or what you think. There is always more of everything you want or need and it is actually closer than you think. No matter if you are just starting out in your art career or starting over, you must believe you have thriving abundance in your Big Picture.

Ask and you Shall Receive

Sometimes you get a taste of success and then lose everything, or at least this is the perception. Build new dreams when you feel you're down to nothing. You build success first through your dreams, desires, and passions. And then, by focusing on them, you attract help and knowledge along the way. However, you must ASK. Why? BECAUSE they're not going to call you! They don't know who you are. YOU HAVE TO REACH OUT. You did that at least once before through the vibration you put out into the world. You can recover, build new dreams and do it again. Keep the faith. Every day is a new beginning and you can start that day over. Every moment offers a new beginning but remember to ask for help.

Allowing your success is an art. Honor your integrity and choose the path of most light. Love getting to the Big Picture as much as being there.

What is your Contentment Level?

You can be as creative or as prosperous as your contentment level is. This is why most folks just get by; that is where they are content; you do have to work to get there and that is a choice.

If you are ready to raise your contentment level, start by being grateful, which expanding your thinking through the use of appreciation for what you already have and what is around you. Choose to uplift and expand your conscious thinking while physically working toward financial independence. Always apply working with unlimited creativity and a good attitude. Do this in both your working and personal relationships. As people in California say, grab the "the whole enchilada." Release through gratitude the abundance that is already YOU. Look around and see what you have to be grateful for. There is always someone who has less than you, so be grateful for what you do have.

An example: When I was a little boy, I saw an artist with no arms who painted amazing pictures with a brush in his mouth. Nothing stopped him from being the artist he wanted to be! Nothing opens the door to success like a thankful, smiling heart. Love and drive can overcome big difficulties.

Drown Out Doubt

Lack of talent and ability are hardly ever the main obstacles to success but doubting your ability to have what you want IS. Get rid of the doubt and affirm your belief in your Big Picture. Every thought and feeling you create permeates your entire body and the energy field around you.

When you doubt your ability to generate the thing you're dreaming of, then you really don't know much about yourself. You are an amazing creation with amazing power flowing through you! Breathing, blood-pumping energy goes in and out. Think about all the energy it takes just to reach out and pick up this book, pick up a pencil and write with it. You're truly an amazing miracle! Think about that. There is infinite power flowing through you; you can do many things with your talent and ability. Think about that; analyze that for a minute. Use affirmations out loud to express what you are capable of accomplishing. Stop doubting your ability and talent. Replace doubt with belief.

The 3 Viewpoints

We basically have three viewpoints in life where our beliefs develop. First, there is a material (external) viewpoint, what we see around us in our environment. Second, there is a spiritual (internal), viewpoint, what we feel at a gut level and the last one is a thought viewpoint, what we gather and formulate opinions from gathering information. Many concentrate exclusively on the third only. However, to be truly successful and balanced, we must heal all three levels of being. This takes patience, love, understanding and kindness.

We are all different and on different paths. What's good for you may not apply to others, so be patient and kind to everyone. Offer assistance when asked for it and don't jam it down anybody's throat as no one likes a zealot. Remember to work on YOU and the right persons, associations and opportunities will be attracted to you naturally and you to them.

To start that attraction is to know what you really want in the first place.

What are your expectations of the persons, companies, galleries you are doing business with? Once again be clear with them.

Chapter Sixteen's Studio Play Sheet

What is your Material (external) viewpoint of success? Write it down.
What is your Spiritual (internal) viewpoint of success? Write it down.
What is your Thought viewpoint of success? Write it down.

_____

What are you happy and grateful for right now? This is your Big Picture right now. Write everything down.

_____

_____

_____

_____

Creative Activity Points

Professional rejection is not personal rejection. Personal rejection is not professional rejection. Do not confuse the two.

The more joyful action you take, the more likely your success will gain mutual professional respect; this energy will be attracted to you as well.

Everything in life gets better when you get better. To get better, you have to think positively, release old thoughts that no longer serve your artistic success, do the work, investigate, emulate, read, research and take action to improve your Big Picture.

Reaching out to others cures loneliness and creates new bonds in both business and friendships.

Reach out to local charities that need your artistry and inspiration.

Reach out to artists who know more by asking for advice.

Reach out to artists who know less by giving appropriate advice.

Seeking a mentor and being a mentor= taking care of your mind and artist spirit self.

CHAPTER SEVENTEEN

See Yourself in The Big Picture

"When one door closes another door opens, but we so often look so long and so regretfully upon the closed door, that we do not see the ones which open for us." —Alexander Graham Bell

Are you afraid of the past? Probably not; the past is over with. Are you afraid of right now? Most likely no, because you're in it and experiencing it right now. So, what are most people afraid of? They have anxiety over the future. Take fear and anxiety out of the future and have some fun creating pictures of how you want your story to become. Then, begin to be grateful for it before you even have it. Nothing cures anxiety and fear like gratitude.

Collages and Vision Boards

When I was in High School, I was given an assignment in art class to make a collage. One of my dreams had always been to move to California when I got out of high school. So, on a collage board I pasted pictures cut from magazines of beautiful places in California: sunny beaches, majestic mountains, beautiful homes, exciting restaurants, cars, and things that made me feel good in general. I posted my collage behind my door in my bedroom. When I came home at the end of the day, I would see my collage board and look at the pictures on it. I did not realize at the time that I was affecting my subconscious mind. Six years later I was living in California, where I wanted, on the beach, driving my new car, and working in a fun job that I had envisioned. I had accomplished everything on my collage.

Today many people use these collages, called vision boards, to instill in their subconscious mind the things they would like to have in their life. I suggest making one. When you look at the picture of the thing you want, on the picture board or even in your mind, think of holding a soft loving puppy, kitten, or fuzzy baby chick and concentrate on a feeling of unconditional love, both given and received.

Create that feeling of love and appreciation in order to attract without putting up invisible walls of which you may be unaware. Make a collage-vision board. Invite friends over and create them together. This creates great energy and excitement. Remember, you are setting up the vibration that calls you and others to action. Think warm puppy and kitty when looking at it. Nice! Feel as if the things on your board are already yours. How does that feel? Are you grateful for even the possibility of knowing that the object of your desire can be yours? Does that feel good? When it does, anxiety goes away. Gratitude and anxiety will not co-exist together. Which one do you prefer?

This book can help you to begin see the Big Picture, but it can't create it for you. You have to do that and, the more you do, the more your art is worth, and the more you are worth. This is where your value begins to accumulate. Now that you know, work with this.

Chapter Seventeen's Studio Play Sheet

Make your Vision Board by yourself or with another. With more than one person, this can be a fun party!

You'll need:

Old magazines and pictures to cut or tear out.
A good size piece of cardboard or poster board for gluing your pictures. A piece 11 x 14 or 16 x 20 inches should be good. Personally, I like 16 x 20.
Paper glue, glue stick or clear tape.
Sticky notes with your symbols on them.

Directions:

1. Cut out pictures of your ideal dream life and start organizing them neatly on your board in an orderly collage. You might have a section for your ideal relationship, home, finances, physical fitness, dream vacation, etc. or you might want to do a vision board for each topic. What's important is to create it and have fun!
2. Make a collage of all the personal and business things you want to do, experience, feel, share, adore and have in your lifetime - put them somewhere you'll see often.
3. Don't put any time constraints on the vision board. Listen for things that point you in the direction of what you have depicted on your vision board.

Help the Vision Out!

As you look at it, change your language; you are in control of what you see there and how you react to it. Don't say, "That's pretty; I'd like to have that someday when I'm richer." Someday when you're richer will never come because that's the energy you're putting out there. In fact, your "someday" will be right now! Knock it off. Say things like, "I just love knowing I do have this or that when I choose to."

Do the same thing when you see cool stuff out in the world. Never be jealous of others because if you choose to, you can have those things and even better ones as you work on your Big Picture.

Creative Activity Points

Creating a collage for personal use it is okay to use all sorts of images without infringing on others rights. It is primarily for your personal development of defining your Big Picture. However should you feel guided to sell your collage or reproduce it for sales it's a very different story. This brings up another issue, other people's rights when creating art. If the collage incorporates other persons intellectual property, licensed or copyrighted material you need permission to sell it and it may be from many entities, from the model, photographer, artist, publishing company, estate, and so on. Permission to reproduce comes in the form of a legal document called a Release in addition to written permission.

When putting others in your art including family members, whether you plan on selling it or not, always get a Signed Model Release Form, from the persons appearing in your art creation. Life changes all the time and no one knows if the future if you will sell the painting or photograph. A signed release limits your liability.

Sometimes real physical property in art also requires a release form as well. Think twice about creating an art piece of someone's private property that could cause embarrassment and legal action. Again common sense reigns supreme. If you did not come up with the original concept then it belongs to someone else. There are areas that can be confusing for example The Hollywood Sign in Los Angeles requires permission from its board of trustees and certain architects and corporations require the same with their buildings. It is unethical to use someone else's work without permission so, before you spend your money make fabulous reproductions of your art inspired from sumptuous cut outs from magazines and articles or famous photographs of your favorite movies star, dead or alive, cartoon or animation characters and sell them for inspiration to others, be sure to get releases from all the owners. You'll need release forms for all of this. The lesson here is: create from your own original concepts.

Create art using your own original creations and avoid a lot of paperwork.

Nothing makes your art boom with success like gratitude.

CHAPTER EIGHTEEN

Tap into Your Power and the Magnificent Power of the Universe

"Trust your own instinct. Your mistakes might as well be your own instead of someone else's." —Billy Wilder

When you exercise your conscious mind though new thoughts, your artist spirit is ignited and excited to bring you new inspiration. So be prepared to receive information. How do you receive it? Through your artist's intuition.

The Artist's Call

Most artists say that deep in their heart, there is something there that tells them that they were born to be artists. They are right. You made an agreement to come here and be the artist, helping others through your beautiful creations. We artists booked the ticket and the wild ride yet we all forget the minute we arrived here. It's so funny when you hear artists say, "I was born to do this." Think about it; you were! Creators were born to come here and create! So why struggle in every direction with being an artist? How do you stop the struggle? Your heart's desire to be an artist wants to rise up and be free.

Dealing with Fear

The struggle is about fear of the unknown and based on early beliefs. These beliefs constantly get reinforced as you go off into the wrong direction. The Earth is bombarded with negative energy. The negative energy is how we get to see what we don't want; it's actually a good thing! However, we get addicted to negative energy and it consumes us in various manifestations.

Follow Your Artist Spirit

You can correct your course and move back into a positive vibe by quieting your artist mind and asking yourself powerful questions. When you raise your vibration of awareness, your inner artist can communicate with you better. Your inner artist, the real you, your soul and spirit are able to be contacted through meditation, writing, prayer and quiet time. Look for answers in ways you understand. Don't expect the mountains to move or the sea to part like in some Hollywood spectacle. Instead, look for subtle changes around you. Be open to new ideas, insights, realizations, new persons with different ideas along your path and synchronistic happenings (those things that seem to land right at your feet). Look and pay attention to a lighter feeling inside. That is your intuition telling you that your artist spirit is around.

You don't have to turn off your mind; that's impossible. However, learn how to quiet your mind so you can hear your heart. Your artist spirit will not interfere with your free will; you have to invite it to interact with what you want. If you are used to struggling, it will allow you to continue to do so. Just ask for help from it when you are ready. There is no right or wrong way to get quiet and invite your artist spirit to come in for guidance. It is important you feel positive and relaxed. Be patient with yourself and let what happens, happen. Keep a record of insightful messages and ideas you receive. They will come when you are relaxed. You can develop a strong connection to your inner artist intuition by learning how to quiet your mind. One way is through meditation and breathing exercises, which we covered earlier in Chapter twelve.

It's your dream to be an artist and you don't need others to approve that. Sharing your positive gains and attitude is enough. Ask your artist spirit why you are here. Ask it what you are to do with your talent? Ask it how your talent can benefit others. Are you here to teach, to share beauty, inspiration, motivation? Are you here to have fun? Be still and keep asking powerful questions like that. What do your inner feelings tell you? Write down your answers. These are your road maps.

As your art career begins to blossom, it is most important that you share your gains, especially with other artists who are starving emotionally. Use compassion and kindness to avoid being pulled back into their drama. There is no need to go there. Just appreciate them for who they are. Send in love and light before you enter a room that may be challenging. Their message says to you that you don't have to be that way and your message says to them that there is a better way.

I recommend that you write down your gains, insights and accomplishments and share them with others. Each time you record your gains and share them, you validate what you've done to benefit yourself. In addition to being a record of your progress, your gains are positive evidence that create momentum and remind you of why you're here and on your artist journey in the first place.

Have you woken up in the middle of the night with a great idea? Did you capture it by writing it down? Or the next day said, "Now, I had this great idea or dream but I forgot what it was…" Great ideas and insights can come to you when you least expect them, and usually from your subconscious team! When these ideas do bubble up, you'll be ready. Write them down immediately and act on your ideas as soon as you can. Keep a spiral notebook by the side of your bed with a pen or pencil. You could title it, "My Million Dollar Idea Book" or whatever you want to call it. Then you can get back to sleep comfortably knowing the idea is out of your mind and onto the paper.

Inspiration Over Lunch

We've all heard great stories recorded on a napkin or receipt, about new inventions, company start-ups, and other ideas that came into being over lunch. I started writing this book an hour after I had lunch with my friend Paul O'Sullivan who asked me how I accomplished what I had done as an artist. He said you have to write book and share this. We immediately wrote down the format and now I can share it with you. You may want to keep a small note pad with you to jot down your spur-of-the-moment great insights as well.

What if you walked up to your mirror and saw a sticky note from God? Would you pay attention if you saw words of encouragement or a great idea? Would you be grateful, excited, freaked out and/or bedazzled? What would it say? Write one.

Do I do this myself? You'd better believe it! Has it paid off for me? You'd better believe it has! I would never suggest any exercise I haven't tried myself.

Just like untapped potential, great ideas in notebooks are useless if they stay there. You must get off your duff and look for ways to turn those ideas into reality. You have a choice to be a big windbag or get a big windfall from your ideas. Take action!

Your problem-solving ability will increase because you know your path. As you practice these exercises you may see a shift in flexibility of your attitudes, as well as those of others. As negative attitudes dissipate a more relaxed and confident artist will begin to emerge. This always brings new accomplishments in the right direction as you open up your creative well.

Tap into your inner artistic guidance and then get to work on your ideas. Taking action based on your intuition is always the very first step in creating a roadmap to success.

Chapter Eighteen's Studio Play Sheet

Practice daily meditation of some sort.

Get a spiral notebook or note pad and keep it by the side of your bed.

Write across the top of it My Million Dollar Idea Art Book.

Enter ideas that come to you in the morning no matter how silly you may think they are. You never know what genius you can tap into at any given moment. After each one, thank your artist spirit.

Write uplifting, encouraging, loving, motivational sticky notes from God, Great Spirit or the Universe notes to yourself and post them on your mirror. Feel free to use humor at times.

Make a simple stick figure image on a sticky note, post it and meditate on the image. Draw the line and reflect on it.

Share your gains and insights with your artist counterparts and customers and be open to new expressions of creativity. I always thought I'd just paint pictures but I've done so much more as an artist including being an author.

Creative Activity Points

You are a powerful and creative being beyond measure. Draw the line in business with your positive or negative thoughts. Use that power responsibly. Trust your heart, intuition and gut instinct; they are your best life guides and they are pure. Send love and gratitude to your ideas and their source. Insist on making your own decisions in your style of art rather than being influenced by the gallery or venue. Find the right venue or create it yourself.

Thank God, the Universe, and your Higher Power daily, even if it's just a quick thank you for your creative individuality. Appreciate your talent. If you don't appreciate your talent while you're alive, how can anyone else?

Everything leaves clues; you do reap what you sow. Read about others who accomplished what you would like, read inspirational books and biographies. Make the time. If you read one inspirational page in a book every morning you'd have read a 365-page book by the end of the year. Sow the seeds of accomplishment through reading and studying the great ones.

Read biographies of persons you would like to emulate.

Be open to new expressions of creativity. Investigate and acquire new skills as you gain more insight on your path.

Increase positive feelings that improve your behavior and attitudes, as this rubs off on your clientele.

Meditation creates greater ease and effectiveness in daily activities.

Allow yourself to release unwanted energy that may block you in many areas of successful living.

Allow for more effective communication with your inner artist spirit.

Provide value and service to others by using the direction you love heightens productivity.

CHAPTER NINETEEN

Asking

"I like a teacher who gives you something to take home to think about besides homework." —Lily Tomlin as "Edith Ann"

Ask, ask, ask, again but ask the right people. Then give it your all!

When venturing off into new territory, job, adventure, or relationship, what are your assumptions? Are they correct? Do you have all the correct information to proceed?

Be open to chart a new course if need be. Sometimes a dead-end job is just that; however, don't run off and start a dead-end business without proper investigation. Hearsay is not proper investigation. To accomplish something you've never done before, step out of your comfort zone and do something different. It's all a risk; be a risk taker *and* use your common sense. In other words, in order to have something you've never had, try something you've never done. Find a role model who has done it and ask them about it. Ask the experts; hire the expert when you can. As you gather information, take notes as you proceed and plant the seeds the expert is sharing with you.

KNOW YOUR STRENGTHS

When artists began asking me for advice I realized I was setting an example for them. When someone told me, "You are just a beacon of information," I decided to found a new company, Beacon Artworks Corporation. The more I learned about what the most successful artists did in their careers, I realized that like them, I would have to be more in control of my destiny if I wanted to have the life I desired. I would have to make a decision and do things I never did before and ask how to proceed and then DO those things. I asked experts how to do what I wanted to do; I hired others to do what I could not or did not want to do so I could focus on my strengths. Often, opposites attract in relationships and that spells success.

My friend, Business Expert Peggy McColl says, "Rather than focus on your limitations and work on your weaknesses, you are better served to focus on your strengths." Hire the experts for tasks where your limitations hold you back from your strengths. When I need to change the oil in my automobile or get my car serviced, not being a mechanic, I take it to an expert to get that job done. We do it all the time. Yet when we start a business, especially one close to the heart, sometimes it's hard to let go and realize there is someone better qualified and waiting to be hired. Often someone will even barter or do for free what you can't or do yourself.

Emulate and Make It Your Own

Find someone who is doing what you dream of and emulate them; learn what you need to do. Find out who they asked and what their system is. Then, create a system for what *you* need to do to, fine tune it and finally, increase your earning potential.

Emulating is a great way to get started. However, all great accomplishments stem from doing something different and better. Focus on your strengths and work with experts where you are weak. Do you think Henry Ford designed and built all those cars by himself? No; he hired experts. Ask, Ask, Ask. I have a friend who owns a thriving hair salon, yet he doesn't cut a single strand of hair or even knows how to; that's what the experts who work for him do.

A Word About Competition

To find success, you can and must blaze your own trail while continuously building upon your own strengths. Once you realize this, you will no longer be worried about the competition because everyone brings their own unique experiences to the table. There is no competition in creating your art. Artists all have separate minds that are untapped reservoirs of genius. What separates the successful artist in business from the rest of the artists is how they apply their business savvy strengths in addition to their art technique,

Set daily, weekly monthly and yearly goals and accomplish them with baby steps, one at a time. Accomplishing a goal is a great feeling, especially when you start keeping record of them. Look back and see your dreams unfold in your own personal story. When you have a business success, like a sale, ask yourself, "What was different in how I presented myself that time over other times when I did not accomplish what I was trying to do?" I guarantee there was a difference somewhere; perhaps in focus, attitude, story, integrity, interest in the customer, something was different in your approach.

Become an expert at delivery. Be organized and gather your information before taking a bold step. Ask the expert, a role model, ask someone who is doing it right; ask if you can take them to lunch or a cup of coffee. It's a risk, but if they say no, you haven't lost anything; you are still right where you were before asking. Ask again. After meeting with your mentor, or expert, send a handwritten thank you note, even flowers if appropriate. It's nice to wow with appreciation.

Calculated Risk Vs. Gambling

Risk taking for the sake of simply taking a risk is not very smart at all; that's called gambling. Calculated risk taking includes investigation and organized planning and is a very smart investment in your future. While you may appear lucky to others, you know you've used common sense and done your homework. Remember the man who bought the bankrupt goldmine and struck it rich? Well, he knew exactly what he was doing.

Have you noticed that most people are always asking advice from, and complaining to, the wrong person? The world is hooked on this. Turn on your TV and the news is doing it in your living room 24 hours a day. You're gleefully paying for them to do it! Be careful what you watch on television, the Internet and where you rebroadcast it in your conversations. When you need advice, go to the source that can give it. If you must complain or right a wrong, go to the person who can assist you in solving the issue.

Are you asking all the right questions? Are you asking all the right questions to the wrong people? Or worse, are you asking the wrong questions to the right people? Are you asking all the right questions to the right people? If you need a raise at work, don't complain to your friends, who can do absolutely nothing about it. If you need your rent reduced, don't complain to your boss about it. Go to the source, the person who can help you.

Many people bury their heads in the sand hoping the problem goes away, yet this just creates more wreckage for themselves and others. If you need assistance with an issue go to the source that can help you.

Are you doing too much? Being overwhelmed from all the action and projects you have piled up, but refusing assistance? We do this all the time without realizing it, except we don't do it for personal projects closest to our hearts. Think about this- while addiction is frowned upon, workaholism can be recognized like a badge of honor. Yet, it's still an addiction. There is a solution to workaholism.

The Solution

When you need a thousand copies of something, you most likely go to the office supply store; you hire them to do a job. You walk in, place the order and hire them for a minute to be part of your team.

Here are some solutions. First and prioritize the things you have to do, and ask why you have to do this or that. Ask yourself, "Why do I have to do these things? Who else could do these things for me?" Take your projects and prioritize what you alone can do and omit the rest.

Build a team and delegate what you cannot or do not need to do. Action can be a trap that leads to procrastination of real issues and workaholism as well.

If the person you entrust the task to needs to delegate, that's their challenge. In other words, get a director of operations first, the first key member of your team besides you. Have only that one director of operations report to you. If they can't get it done, that's their problem. They may have to hire someone to work for them; that's no longer your responsibility. If your appointee can't pull it off, perhaps you'll need to search for a new director of operations. There is a difference between being busy and being productive. You must use discernment and prioritize your action. You must have quality time in life for yourself and family.

Self-Reflection is Key

To find better ways of doing things, ask empowering questions of yourself, as well! Ask good ones, especially before you go to bed such as, "Why I am now a multi millionaire?" or "What is the thing that I did to accomplish my goal?" You mind is a marvelous computer and when you sleep, it will search for answers to your intriguing questions; pay attention to the answers. It's not uncommon that they just pop up out of the blue. This means you also have to be listening for answers..

Set It Free!

I've had some pretty cool things happen with my art. People ask me all the time, "How did you do that?" Well, I did the footwork, the creative, fun part for me and then I let it go. I asked for assistance and advice from experts that did *their* footwork, the creative, fun part for them. Then, if needed, they brought the art to the next level of experts or team until the Big Picture for each expert was reached. These co-creators always deliver a much bigger picture than I could have ever dreamed up when stepping up to my blank canvas. I just know in my heart that everything and everyone has the power within to be very special.

Be willing to make your art and then set it free. Do not give your art away haphazardly or just to anybody for when you do that, you set yourself up to be victimized. Release it through licensing or a detailed sales contract, and then realize that it belongs to the world, taking on a life of its own.

There are many types of experts that can take your creations to the next level, including other artists. They will help turn your art into many productive and beautifully inspiring things that you don't have the time or expertise to do on your own. Let them do this through the proper channels. Use your common sense, protect your creative rights and let it go. Let your art work for you first and work for others next. The rewards will come. That is the blessing and magic of art. Art keeps creating art. With it, you could be creating jobs, feelings, dialogue, wealth, freedom, new aspiring artists and unlimited possibilities!

Not knowing gets you nowhere in any situation. Ask, ask, ask and listen, listen, listen then give it your all, and let the experts give it their all, as well!

Chapter Nineteen's Studio Play Sheet

Ask yourself, *Do I really want to change?*

Focus on your strengths and seek expert advice in whatever area your weaknesses lie.

Find role models in the areas of life that you seek change or improvement. Hire them if need be.

Enlist the help of your mastermind group for resources.

Actively practice these new exercises and shatter old habits.

Search out and locate a professional who is living your dream. Do not waste their time; have your questions ready (write them a letter, send them an e-mail and ask him/her for advice). Be sure to thank them when you receive a response.

Research and study role models who have lived your dream; what did they do to achieve their success? Ask yourself if their strengths are similar to yours.

Ask friends and associates what life repeating patterns they see that you may be unaware of. Negative and Positive!

Schedule appointments with people you want to ask questions of. Never just show up.

When you do show up, always show up on time.

Never waste time on old business. If it should come up in conversation, courteously change the subject and move on.

Make no commitments that you do not intend to fully keep; say no without hesitation to things that waste your time and muddy your Big Picture.

License the usage of your art to professional, ethical business entities; then get out of the way and let them work their magic.

Creative Activity Points

You do not have to do everything. You can't and frankly, sometime you shouldn't.

Hire professionals who know more than you in certain areas and who have fun doing the things you do not like to do such as sales, contracts, finance, law, marketing etc.

When looking for your first employee, look for a Director of Operations. He/she reports directly to you; everyone else will report to them.

Do business with decision makers. If the person you are talking to can't make a call on something, you're talking to the wrong person. Thank them and find out who you need to do business with.

Keep appointments and confirm all of them.

Use common sense first. Always sell or license the rights with details explaining the rules of usage when you ask experts for help.

Only seek advice from artists who are more successful in business than you. If you don't know any, this is telling you something. People need role models. Could you be mentoring others?

You can sell more than just your physical art; you can sell talking about it, speaking and lecturing to other people who are asking for knowledge, insight and inspiration as well.

Once you have your appointment confirmed, step up to the counter and ask for what you want.
Ask people if they know other talented people who can work with you.
Rather than advertising, invest in the recruitment of talented co-creators and employees.
Ask for the sale.

STUDIO SIX

Investigate Inspiration

Step Six: Be Integrity Grounded

Find, Investigate and Live Your Passions
Follow and Map Out Your Inspirations
Make a Contribution with Vision Through Action

CHAPTER TWENTY

Wake Up and Dream

"The most pathetic person in the world is a person who has their sight but no vision."—Helen Keller

KNOWING YOUR HEART'S DESIRE AND REMEMBERING THE FUTURE

What do you really want; what is your vision? What are your heart's desires and passions? What makes your heart skip a beat when you discuss or think about it? What is it that makes your heart sing? The feeling you have when you think of those things creates a powerful vibration. When you act on that vibration, your potential becomes amplified. You deserve to live the best life ever, so before we go any further, give yourself all the permission to be and do what you desire and want. We are going to explore what you want. Detach and surrender to your artist Highest Good and learn how to do what you love for your livelihood and the likelihood of others. Follow your inspirations to make a contribution to a brilliant future. Use your talents.

Passion, more than any other emotion including fear, is born from your heart's desire and drives you to succeed where the odds are stacked against you. Passion is what defines you, it creates your attraction to others and what initiates your legacy. Passion is what keeps you curious about your partners, your work, your life and it's what keeps you young at mind and heart.

By discovering your future passions you create new direction in your life, which allows new prosperity to flow into life for yourself and others. This discovery supports your dreams and creates prosperity for you, as well others, by supporting their dreams. When you know what your passion is, you can now take on commitments by saying 'yes' to those things that are in alignment with your future passion. Hopefully, you're saying 'no' to the things that are not lining up with your Big Picture. The knowledge of your future is the discovery of your highest purpose and should be your first priority in daily activities. From those passions you create new goals. From those goals create a daily to-do list, which is in alignment with your heart's desires. When you do what you love life moves along happily and you set a great example for yourself and others to follow. Is your art's desire your heart's desire?

It's all in your Mind

If your thoughts and feelings create things, it is futile to complain about what could have been. The same goes for thinking or saying how foolish you or others are, as well. Let's say you won the lottery. Look at the statistics of lottery winners. It's pretty bleak, at best. Most wind up losing everything and eventually going bankrupt. Why? Because of an ongoing lack mentality; they weren't ready or prepared to accept the windfall of prosperity into their subconscious mind. They weren't ready for a fortune mentally or emotionally. That's okay, that doesn't have to be your journey, so don't let it be. As mentioned in other chapters, develop the mindset to receive the success you want and see yourself as already having it.

If you had the ability to snap your fingers and go back in time to change things, it would still be difficult to predict how those things would unfold. Looking back, is there something you would have changed if you could? Looking forward to where you want to end up, is there something you could change today to get there? Why not do some investigating?

Perhaps you might be able to start that change right now. If thoughts and feelings create things then perhaps letting go and releasing old thoughts and feelings can make room to create new, better ones. Actually, that's exactly what can be done. Wake up and dream; living right now is what matters.

Be a TV Host

Always embrace a consuming passion by lovingly sharing it with others. Be enthusiastic. My heritage is Italian and we have a reputation for being fun-loving, expressive people who talk a lot with our hands. Try it; practice expressive talking with your hands when talking about your art masterpieces and other things you love.

Have you watched those reality shows where somebody wins a chance to be a TV host of their own show? When they describe things, they use their hands a lot. Be a TV host. Have one of your friend's video record you presenting your art work; then, review the video and see if it's exciting to watch. Keep making it over until it's great. Then, upload it to the Internet and put a copy on your website. Get excited when you tell stories about your creations; you'll sell more. Surround yourself with others who share your passion and you'll find they fuel your enthusiasm and together you can create amazing projects. These days it's all about creating together and in order to do this, you must identify your passion.

Laziness

Often you hear artists say, "I have to be in the mood to make my art" or "If I lived in a place like you, I'd be inspired too." This one is classic- "When I retire from the job that's holding me hostage, I'll become the artist I am." Artists tell me this everyday. They say that they have to wait for the right moment to be inspired, as if they think they are waiting for the sky to part, the angels to sing and be struck by lightning. Do you have to be inspired to make your art? Are you waiting until retirement to do the creative things you have wanted to do all your life? Have you bought into that story? That 'waiting around until you feel like it' attitude comes from bad childhood programming that turned into a belief. When you say, "I don't feel like it today," guess what? You'll feel less and less like doing it and before you know it, your art career has gone derelict. Laziness births a starving artist mentality and gives you a sloppy reputation.

Grandma Moses

Do you know of Anna Mary Robertson Moses? She liked to do needlepoint but in her seventies it was becoming too painful due to arthritis, so she began painting pictures. Painting became her passion. Her paintings are what critics call primitive, which is a nice way of saying 'untrained and childlike,' but that doesn't matter. She became a world renowned artist while she was alive, commanding competitive prices from her pieces, which today are in private collections and museums all over the world. She didn't worry about taking another class for technique, being in the mood or feeling better; she did what she loved and she shared her passion with everyone. She lived to the ripe old age of one hundred and the world knows her as Grandma Moses, an American treasure.

Start everyday with a clean slate. You have the ability to be creative and change your mood in the snap of a second. Start the day by reading or listening to something inspirational. There are so many easily available resources. Sign up for an inspirational message everyday from countless websites. Switch out bad thoughts by affirming good ones and get the creative, inspired juices going in the right frequency. Then, get into action again, step up to your blank canvas and go for it. Contact the right people and go for it. End the day by reading something inspirational too. Go to sleep inspired.

There's a treasure trove of buried untapped brilliance six feet under the ground because some folks never got around to being in the mood to be inspired. Don't sink your ship with doubt, procrastination or complacency. Remember, you are the captain in control of your life, your ship. Though it's never too late, waiting until you retire is a ridiculous goal. Do you now what they do with retired ships? They mothball them, sink them, or sell them for scrap. Ships that just sit there in the bay rot when they are unused. A good question to ask of yourself is, "Do I really want to make a living with my art?" If yes, why wait? If you just want to do art as a hobby, that's fine too, but have respect for yourself as a hobbyist and don't obsess about being a professional or waste other professionals' time either. If you are retired and want to start a new career, go for it!

Most gallery owners, collectors and other artists I've spoken with tend to believe that the majority of artists are moody, flaky or just plain lazy. Perhaps that's why Hollywood dramatizes and idolizes the struggling artist. In reality, everyone behind the scenes and in front of the camera is working their tail off, finding a way to get their inspiration on the silver screen. Think about that. Now don't go and blame Hollywood for your predicaments. It's easy to cop out and point the blame. Take charge of your life.

If dramatic struggle in the arts is your belief, you can change that image starting with your own inspiring daily action. Waiting around until you "feel like it" or to be "in the mood" is the worst way to be creative and achieve your Big Picture. Tomorrow never comes. What's your Big Picture? What are you going to do today to get inspired, be in the mood and make it happen?

Learn to embrace risk. Wake up to your dream. A way to shift your perspective is to see risk as dashing into the future with hope and the possibility to move closer to an impersonal goal and greater purpose. What is the worst thing that could happen if you follow your passion or heart's desire? Being no better off than where you are right now? Always wondering 'what if'? Don't wait for luck; that's the ego's make-believe friend. Believe in risk and ask, "What's the best thing that could happen?" Some may suggest this is wishful thinking; however wishful thinking combined with persistent dedicated action is how dreams materialize into reality. Can you picture it?

Lessons from the Family Business

Earlier, I mentioned that we see things in pictures and then create pictures in our mind. I was fortunate enough in my late twenties to benefit from gaining knowledge from my family-run businesses. They were in the photo processing business, and I learned marketing, customer service, accounting and human resources which later I learned could each individually be sources of income generation.

There at the shops, I learned about selling and providing valuable service. At all our locations we provided value not just though our physical product but also through another very important service, confidentiality. Before the days of digital processing, our business did that for the client. We processed photographs for some of the wealthiest and most famous families on the planet.

Business Grows Where Integrity Flows

One of the earlier business tips I mentioned in this book was- business grows where integrity flows. We had an unspoken rule: never release, share or talk about anyone's privacy, especially his or her pictures. Because of this trust, we established a personal one-on-one rapport with most of the customers, dealing with most of them directly. They, in return, shared their experiences with me. It was fascinating!

On more than one occasion, a competitor opened their doors across the street. They offered lower-priced products and promised to deliver in half the time. Within six months to a year they were usually gone. Business Grows where Integrity Flows. Never underestimate the value of service, integrity and trust. The pictures in your mind will lead you forward to a bigger picture, as big as you want it to be. Others may have experienced some of the very things you want to and often are happy to share their inspiring Big Picture advice with you.

Keep customer confidences and when you do, your customers will market your product for you. They are your best salespeople.

There is no better symbol to portray to the world with your business than being a symbol of trust.

Night on the Town

I speak a lot about using symbols and seeing in pictures so I want to share with you about how I learned about that. When I was a young man in my early twenties out on the town, I met another young artist and we had a brief conversation about art and being artists. This man told me he wanted to be a famous artist and he was going to be. I asked how he planned on doing that. He told me two important things that I never forgot and that was to "be of service with your art from your heart" and "people see in pictures and understand symbols." A few weeks later I ran into him on the street in New York City selling his T-Shirts on the sidewalk where I had to have one. Something inside me told me he was special and his t-shirt creation was also, so I never wore it; I just treasured it. I am so thankful for his wisdom everyday and his advice helped my own career in the arts tremendously. Within a short time of telling me those things this artist did indeed see his art career reach phenomenal heights. His name was Keith Haring, and though he left us way too soon, his art changed an entire generation and brought awareness to the human condition through the symbols he created. Thank You Mr. Haring!

Chapter Twenty's Studio Play Sheet

Remember the future and paint a Big Picture of the direction you are headed.

1. As quickly as you can, write down a list of one through 20 of your heart's desires. To do this finish the end of this next sentence 20 times. "When I am living my ideal life I am…." (Use action words such as: living, traveling, climbing, exercising, building, praying, teaching, etc...)

Do not worry what you will write; write the answers quickly. You might be surprised what comes through. Many folks find they are already achieving some of their heart's desires and some find new and unexpected things pop up! I know they did for me. Let your thoughts flow out of you quickly and non-judgmentally. You can always go back and change them; there is no wrong way to do this.

2. When your list is done, go back and identify which sentence is most important. Starting with sentence number one. Is that desire more important than the second? If not, is that desire more important than the third? Keep going down the list eliminating the least from the most important desires. It's sort of like taking the vision test at the eye doctor except this is the vision for the future! Continue all the way down to the bottom of the list until you have your top FIVE hearts' desires.
3. Write those FIVE heart's desires down on five different index cards and place them in strategic places around your home, car, and work. Write them down on a business card and carry them with you in your wallet.
4. Write on the top of a separate page each heart's desire. Write down ten goals that need to happen in order for you to achieve your heart's desire your ideal artist life.

This next part is going to take more time.

5. When you are finished with the first heart's desire list, use a separate piece of paper to write what you must do in order to achieve this heart's desire.
What would you have to do in five years in order to achieve your heart's desire?
What would you have to do in four years to achieve your heart's desire?
What would you have to do in three years to achieve your heart's desire? Two years? One year? Six months? One month? Two weeks? Tomorrow?
6. Do whatever that thing might be; write it on your to-do list for tomorrow. Take your time, contemplate and write down everything. This exercise alone could change your life. It's changing mine as you read this.

My Big Picture Desire List

When I am living my ideal artist life, I am….
_____

When I am living my ideal artist life, I am….
_____

When I am living my ideal artist life, I am….
_____

When I am living my ideal artist life, I am….
_____

When I am living my ideal artist life, I am….
_____

When I am living my ideal life, I am….
_____

When I am living my ideal artist life, I am….
_____

When I am living my ideal artist life, I am….
_____

When I am living my ideal artist life, I am….
_____

When I am living my ideal life, I am….
_____

When I am living my ideal artist life, I am….
_____

When I am living my ideal artist life, I am….
_____

When I am living my ideal artist life, I am….
_____

When I am living my ideal artist life, I am….
_____

When I am living my ideal artist life, I am….
_____

When I am living my ideal artist life, I am….
_____

When I am living my ideal artist life, I am….
_____

When I am living my ideal artist life, I am….
_____

When I am living my ideal artist life, I am….
_____

When I am living my ideal artist life, I am….
_____

My Top FIVE Artist's Desires
Transfer From the list above your top five Artist Heart's Desires

When I am living my ideal artist life, I am….

1.

2.

3.

4.

5.

This is My Big Picture!

Now, create your art and your career goals to complement what is on your list. Your heart's desire is your art's desire as well. You can make decisions based on whether they are in agreement with your top desires. These all help you steer closer to your Big Picture. Do these exercises every six months or so to see if you have new desires you'd like to investigate as your big picture expands.

One-on-One

You can do another powerful exercise with a friend. Find quiet time and a quiet place. Sit across from one another and for a solid five minutes each person asks, "What do you really want?" of the other person. Do not interrupt; just keep asking for a full five minutes. You might record it and or take notes for each other. Your answers may surprise you, so do it with a person you feel comfortable with.
Create a Vision Board of Your Top Five Ideal Artist Desires

Creative Activity Points

You don't have to know what your business will bring in the future to be certain about the present. Make sure you're doing what you want to be doing with your art business right now.

Do not lose your personal artistic vision. Keep track of it with this exercise and revise it if need be. Never jeopardize what could have been.

When you wake up and before you start the day, read or listen to something inspirational that relates to your Big Picture.

The willingness to give it your all will lead you in the direction of having it all. Never underestimate the value of service and trust you provide.

Allow persons to share their experiences with you. Let this ignite your inspiration. Be grateful for these angels, as they are guides pointing the way to your Big Picture.

Be nice to all persons as you climb up and down and all around the ladder of success. You never know whom you pass in either direction! It's a Big Picture, but it's also a small world.

Sign gallery agreements stating that you are to be informed of customer identity and must receive their contact information when they purchase your art piece. If galleries are not willing to provide this information to you, they are undercutting your commission price and overcharging the customer. You should always know who your customer is. The gallery works for the artist, not the other way around.

Sign all agreements with galleries and exhibition places before you leave your art with them. You should always know what will be done with your art, how will be displayed, where it will be stored, how you will be paid and in how many days after it is sold. Fifteen days or less is appropriate.

Always keep your customer list confidential between you, the gallery and the customer. Not your friends, the local paper or the evening news.

Never charge less than the gallery that carries your art. When you undercut the gallery who sells for you, this creates a damaging reputation to you and the gallery. It hurts the gallery's customer base. Remember, the customer is investing in you and your art as well.

Open your own gallery if you are better at selling your work than anyone else.

You must know what price your art is selling for at public market and your private prices must reflect that as well.

Some galleries will buy your art outright. You must know what they are selling it for. Your prices should reflect their selling price as well.

When galleries buy your art outright, you are probably underpriced and a very good artist.

CHAPTER TWENTY ONE

Make Space

"Have nothing in your houses that you do not know to be useful or believe to be beautiful." —William Morris

A cluttered house is like a cluttered mind, full of confusion and disorganization. Unlike the Law of Attraction we hear so much about, we don't hear about another vital law, yet they go hand-in-hand. It is referred to as the Vacuum Law of Prosperity.

Here's how it works: Go to the back yard and dig a hole. Leave it alone and you will find that it won't be very long before the hole starts to fill itself with new dirt. After some time goes by, there will be only an indentation where there once was a hole.

It works the same way for you, as well. If your home office is cluttered, how can you possibly have room for new opportunity to come in? This applies to material things, relationships and your life in general. There must be room for what you want or what you want to happen; there must be space for it.

Do you have so much 'stuff' in your studio that you could fill a gallery of your own? Have you set up the business with future expansion in mind for 'someday?' Are you physically stockpiling and justifying things at home instead of getting on with business?

An example:

A few years back, I was talking to a friend who wanted desperately to have a new love relationship. Meanwhile, his closets were jammed with clothes, many of which haven't been worn in years. His nightstand was stacked to the rafters and I won't even mention all the things stored under the bed!

How can you have room for "him or her" to come into your life if there's no place for "him or her" to come into? How can the Universe respond to your desires if you haven't made room for what you want?

When I said these same things to him, he vehemently argued that "THEY" should be making room for ME!" He continues to be single.

A common argument with just about everything today is "it's them – not me". Is it any wonder that you get stuck? Lots of our "overstocking" mentality is attributable to a generationally embedded and inherited habit that comes from our parents, their parents, teachers, and other role models who have been through tough times and learned to stock up. "There are starving people in the world; finish everything on your plate; who do you think you are asking for something new? We can't afford it; you should be happy with what you have." The list goes on. Fear of not having enough causes squirrels, chipmunks and some humans to hoard for the cold winters ahead. After all, no one wants to be a 'starving' artist.

Hoarding creates more lack mentality. I've seen it in my own family. With that said, what's under that bed, in the attic, basement or storage shed? Are you paying a storage fee for stuff you haven't used in over a month with no plans of using it in the near future? "Is it out of sight – out of mind, or are you out of YOUR mind? This probably means you don't need the hidden stuff in the first place. So, what are you stockpiling for? Are you filling a void with stuff instead of dealing with what's really missing in your life? Tally the cost of your unused stuff and you will be shocked. You could put that money to good use earning compounding interest or to start your new business, go on your dream vacations, enroll in classes, you name it! However, don't beat yourself up over that at all; just get to work and don't clutter the closets, office, or shelves anymore. Get rid of these stockpiles and the storage unit you haven't taken a look at in ages. Someone else needs it more. Clean up your traffic jam and let the good you deserve begin to flow to you now.

Whenever you say to yourself, "I could use this someday," think twice; someday usually never comes. That little voice popping in is our old belief system that's just not ready for the new miracles to come in to our lives. You can change that. See The Big Picture.

Chapter Twenty-One's Studio Play Sheet

Use the Vacuum Law of Prosperity to attract and magnetize what you want.

Don't wait for spring-cleaning! Do it now.

Take your old stuff that's been hiding in the dark and bring it into the light and let it become someone else's treasure. Take it to Goodwill, the Salvation Army or donate it to a local charity drive. You will feel great! You might even get a tax write-off as well, depending upon where you live. Just get going and lighten up your load!

Clean out your closets, cabinets and cubbyholes now! Start with one bagful a week, until your closet is half empty! Don't sell the stuff; give it to charity, to someone who deserves it. Thank all those things for serving you well and release them. This gets the gratitude flowing!

Fill your mind with inspiring books, articles, movies, friendships etc. Don't clutter it with junk!

Creative Activity Points

If it's in storage, it can't make you a living; however, it can cost you money, peace of mind and valuable selling space.

Clean out the stuff you don't need and get rid of it! Give it away. Someone needs it more than you do and they will be grateful to have it.

When you release the abundance of things you have, look at the value you placed on the items when you got them. Thank them for serving their purpose. They have.

Before spending your money on things you will pack away again, ask yourself if it will serve your higher purpose and be an investment in your life and art career.

Take a breather from over spending in your home and mind.

The more value you give unconditionally, the more you'll have to share. Share your expertise lovingly.

The willingness to give it all up will lead you in the direction of having it all.

Before signing a commercial lease at the 'perfect' place in the neighborhood, learn about leases; there are different types. You want the most cost-effective space located where your customer base shops. If your customers aren't there, you could go out of business and still be liable for the whole life of the lease.

Work with a commercial real estate agent who is working for YOU, not the landlord.

Investigate books and information on lease negotiating. Preparation is key.

Take baby steps. You may be content working from home, as are many art entrepreneurs.

Always cover your tail, get liability insurance, sign legal agreements with artists you represent, as well and keep good records.

CHAPTER TWENTY TWO

Set the Stage

"One man's daydreaming is another man's day." —Grey Livingston

Set the Stage for Success with a combination of meditation and vision. The first time I visualized, I manifested an art show in Los Angeles. I was not a starving artist so to say, but I was hungry to offer my services.

I got my very first art exhibit at a café because another artist didn't show up. Hungry, I walked in to have lunch and to review the little art portfolio I carried under my arm. I walked out with an art show and a full stomach. Today, I am a well-established and sought after artist and that café is long gone. I'll likely never find out what happened to the other artist who didn't show. For all I know, their art could have been better in some way and more beautiful, however, I was the one who persisted and showed up. Because of suiting up and showing up, I reaped the rewards that followed: dedicated collectors, good publicity and acceptance into more prestigious galleries and places of exhibition. Someone's failure to show became an opportunity and a gold mine for me. Here's what happened-

I remember the first time I visualized and manifested an art show in Los Angeles. I was not a starving artist per se, but it seemed I was getting nowhere in offering my art services.

Nothing was turning up as I searched for places to show my artwork, but I continued to keep the faith; I knew a space would eventually appear somewhere. Doors always opened when I followed my "gut" feelings. To my knowledge, I had never consciously visualized before, however, this day I did just that.

One morning after recently moving to Los Angeles, I decided to act **as if** I already had an art show on the books and needed to deliver my paintings to the gallery. Mind you, I had no art show lined up. Loading up my old blue Toyota with twenty little paintings, I acted **as if** my show was real. I fired up my chariot and headed into the big city like a gladiator with a packed arena awaiting me. I stopped at a few gallery spots, and to my surprise, none of them were open. Disappointing? But, I was determined to continue my quest and was grateful to be living in sunny Southern California again.

By two o'clock that afternoon, I pulled the car over; I was tired, a bit overwhelmed and my stomach growled. Thankfully, I had packed a snack. Sitting in my car wondering what to do next, and with a clear picture in my head of exactly what I wanted, I decided to play a game with myself.

The Play in my Mind

This game came from a childhood memory. As I mentioned before, I grew up in the small town and next door to our house was a country playhouse where Summer-Stock Theater came every year. I loved watching the shows and actors transform from rehearsal to opening night. As "the kid next door," I was often invited to see the show for free. Those memories gave me a thought. Closing my eyes, I saw in my mind a beautiful old theater and inside taking place was a production of my successful art opening, titled "My Art Exhibit." The curtain went up and I saw myself in the scenes, making paintings, delivering and hanging them at the gallery. In the next scene came opening night. I saw myself surrounded by friends, enjoying great food, conversation and taking cash and checks from buyers. Smiling, I ended the little play in my mind's eye, feeling quite accomplished, hearing the big curtains close to applause, and myself saying aloud "The End." I clapped my hands, opened my eyes and let my vision go. Feeling nice and relaxed, I looked up and noticed a cute little café called "Carolyn's" a few doors down. I needed food and the place looked great, so I grabbed my portfolio to review it over lunch.

I walked into the cafe and the woman behind the counter asked, "Are you the artist?"

"Yes," I answered. My *goodness! How did she know that? Are all these folks in L.A. psychic*? I wondered. "The artist's here!" she hollered to her boss in the backroom of the café.

The manager yelled back, "It's about time," looking out from the back room and said, "He's not the artist!" You see, as it turned out, the artist they'd lined up for an exhibit never appeared. In fact, days had passed and those café walls were looking bare. "Do you have art with you now?" the manager asked me firmly. "Oh yes!" I answered, handing over my portfolio, and running to my car, where my paintings were ready to hang!

The manager looked at my portfolio and said, "These are beautiful; lets hang your art right now and let me buy you lunch. You know, artists come in all the time wanting shows. They seem to have great potential, but they do not follow through. If you can follow through, then show your art here as long as you like; when something sells, you'll bring in another to keep the place looking full. Do you want an opening party? You get people here; I'll take care of the food. I don't want a commission, just beautiful art on our walls for my customers to enjoy while eating my food."

Wow! My own little gallery complete with opening night, fine food, and centrally located in Los Angeles! Okay, it wasn't the space I expected, but let me tell you, I didn't have to think twice before I accepted the offer. I said 'yes' right away. The next weekend, we were enjoying my art opening complete with delicious food, friends and buyers!

What happened to me that day? I wasn't the artist who was supposed to show up. I got an art show and made a local business happy. Not to mention, my hungry belly was fed with a delicious lunch. I visualized with intention, made a game out of it, sent strong positive and powerful "creative emotions" out into the Universe. I was aware, paid attention, and acted on that awareness and what it presented. Then, I followed through with a decision, one that I am sure changed my life for the better.

Manifestation Playhouse

I suited up and showed up for the life of my dreams! And you can too. I use this technique with those I mentor; we call it "Manifestation Playhouse." Set the stage and try it for yourself.

By playing Manifestation Playhouse a few minutes daily, you can slowly increase your positive vibration to where you want it to be and implant in your subconscious mind the feeling of achieving your wanted desires. This tool is much more than wishful or positive thinking because when you play "a game," your ego steps out of the way and quiets down. The ego cannot be bothered with those silly games; its job is much too dramatic and would rather feed on fear and uncertainty. This "play" exercise will create subtle shifting in your energy, using upbeat positive images to maintain a good vibration in attracting what you wish to accomplish.

Just as in anything, baby steps and balance will eventually lead to bigger steps and further success. So keep track of your positive evidence. A vibrational change is a process that is best not rushed. That little show at the café turned out to be perfect venue for the service I could offer at the time. By saying 'yes' to what manifested before me, more business career doors opened, which eventually led to me living the artist life of my dreams: connecting with excellent patrons, galleries and museum shows, being published many times and eventually founding my art-based companies.

When we decide what we want, individually and collectively, there is no limitation. The Universe recognizes our desire and immediately begins to deliver it to us. Whether we're an artist or non-artist, be open to receive a sparkling life with rave reviews. Identify your desire and then take steps to fulfill the outcome. Do you have service to offer? Are you ready to set your stage? If you said yes, good! Take these tools in this story and like a director in a play, shout out, ONE, TWO, THREE … Action!

Chapter Twenty-Two's Studio Play Sheet

Take the previous story you wrote about yourself one hundred years from now from the exercise in Chapter 15 and apply Manifestation Playhouse to it. If you haven't written that story yet, do so now. When you are done, proceed.

Be as quiet as you are for meditation.

Close your eyes and take deep breathes. Envision yourself walking up to a beautiful old theater and on the marquee is reflected your name and story. As you walk in, you notice that the posters on the wall also indicate the show name, exhibit, movie, etc. and your name is on the playbill.

You walk into the grand old lobby and then into the theater. You find the perfect seat and have the theater all to yourself. The lights dim and the curtains go up. The orchestra plays and we are about to see the production of your Life Story.

Create the perfect storyline in your mind. What would you like to see happen? Which fabulous actors play the parts? The story can be as long or as short as you want to make it. This is your perfect dream story. If you like, you can rewrite it. You are the writer and the director because after all, it's about YOU.

When the play is over and the curtain closes, clap your hands and open your eyes. You have just played Manifestation Playhouse, a very powerful visualization exercise.

Where did you see yourself?

Who was the actor playing you? Was it someone else? Or was it you?

What exciting scenes unfolded before your eyes?

Did something new and unexpected happen?

Did you know precisely what story would unfold; did you focus on that?

Did what you want to accomplish in life take place on stage or was this storyline entirely different? Write down any new insights you may have had and take measures to investigate them.
EVERYTHING IS IMPORTANT AND EVERYTHING MATTERS in every area of your life.

Creative Activity Points

In order for you to have your dream life, you must suit up and show up for it every day.

Having positive emotions increases the magnetism for artistic prosperity to flow towards you. Be positively creative with your imagination.

Artistic success comes in many forms; prepare wisely and set the stage for it.

No one can possibly know everything needed to make your art business successful. Talk to your lawyer, accountant, banker, and also get advice from entrepreneurs more successful than you who have suited up and survived all sorts of business climates.

Create a board of advisors, who can include members of your mastermind team. Be sure that your advisory meetings are held on a regular basis once a month or so. Bounce ideas off each other. Give advisors an incentive for participating, such as a signed print or little original art piece that is special and just for them. Sincere appreciation and gratitude go far.

Be generous with your goodwill. Successful companies share their wealth with key customers and charitable organizations. You don't have to give away the house, however. You can show your support with integrity and love through volunteering as well.

Should you decide to hire an employee, be sure to reward him/her as well. Money and raises are nice, however, motivation can come from other sources, such as profit sharing and celebration of their participation in your success. Before setting the stage in real life, always sign contracts with the entity to which you are releasing your work. There are plenty of Artist-Gallery contracts out there to review.

CHAPTER TWENTY-THREE

Make a Big "To Do" Over Tomorrow

"One today is worth two tomorrows; never leave that till tomorrow which you can do today." —Benjamin Franklin

Good organization is the key to making a living as an artist, but it can also be time consuming and exhausting at first if you're not used to it. Many people waste valuable time working on their "To Do" lists for the day first thing in the morning. Don't waste that early morning time making exhausting lists. Create your "To Do" list for the next day at the end of each day.

Do you have so many things to do that nothing ever gets done? Is "being busy" distracting you from what you really want to do with your art? Perhaps you really don't want to do you art. That's something important to think about. We've explored what we want and don't want. Is there something about art or the business of art that makes you miserable? Why do I ask this? Because I see a lot of frustration in people who spent a ton of money going to school for a fine arts degree and then wind up in a profession they hate, even when the job is art-related.

I have noticed this with some art teachers and gallery owners.

Let me ask you some questions. What do you do on your day off? Besides catching up on rest and doing nothing, how do you spend your time in the morning? Do you spend time with your nose in the paper or online reading the news? If so, what captures your attention every time? Politics? Arts? The Business Section? Entertainment? Science? Fashion? Sports? Real Estate? Those areas of current events you are always sticking your nose in are big clues to where you may find your gold mine using your art. These subjects are your areas of interest that could benefit others!

Take yourself on a date. If you took yourself on a date, where would you go and what would you do? Could you spend getting to know yourself rather than be distracted by "being busy?" P.S.: Sitting on the couch glued to the television eating junk food may be a nice try but that's not a date.

Your dreams are a BIG DEAL. Don't let anything or anyone turn them into a small picture because they will if you allow them to. Go after your dreams with tenacity. Make time for them and get stuff out of the way to free up your time.

Tackle the biggest and most uncomfortable "To Do" first and get it done and over with each day. This will ease up the workday and get so much accomplished that you will surprise yourself.

Creating your "To Do" list the day before provokes your subconscious mind to creatively solve your tasks at hand while you sleep. Upon awakening be ready to start accomplishing goals on your list. Keep this valuable exercise ongoing. Tasks that don't get completed today get carried over to your list this evening and go to the top of tomorrow's "To Do" list.

Again, make tomorrow's list at your desk and leave it there. Leave work on time. Don't take your work home with you or in your mind.

Here's another reason why the early "To Do" works. Don't let anyone or especially, your ego, fool you. No one respects a sacrificing worker who stays late on the job. It always appears they can't get their job done in the time frame allotted. The ego tells the worker he/she is so fabulous, self-sacrificing, dedicated and under-appreciated, so you'll show them! Instead, get in to work early and wow them first thing while everyone is figuring out their "To Do" list for the day. You'll be nearly done with your necessary tasks and will be available for other important duties that come up. Be prepared. Make your "To Do" list the day before but don't forget to have compassion for the folks staying late.

Chapter Twenty-Three's Studio Play Sheet

Do your " To Do" list for tomorrow at the end of your workday today, at your office, or at home before you go to sleep. You'll sleep better!

Creative Activity Points

Go into work early to get things done when you're fresh from a good night's sleep.

Learn to express compassion in business while holding yourself and others to high standards. Be respectful; we're all in this together yet we are all on our own unique paths.

Read inspirational passages first thing in the morning and last thing at night.

Before contracting with a gallery for representation, always agree on exhibition expenses up front, including shipping to and from, insurance and packaging. Write down whom you spoke with and the time and date.

Get your checklists for what you want from the gallery, promoter, and exhibit space ready before you get the show so there are no surprises afterwards.

If you have a solo or group exhibit, get in writing the time, place and location of the show. Make a separate folder with checklist inside for each venue.

Agree on commissions based on the gallery sale price charged to the buyer and sign an agreement that allows you or your representative to inspect their books during any business hours of operation.

Galleries should furnish artists with accounting records a minimum of every 90 days of their on-hand art and the artist should be paid within 30 days after a sale.

Galleries should always be liable for loss or damage to the artist's work. Do not sign a waiver. They carry liability insurance. If they don't want to do this, ask yourself if you really want to leave them with your art.

Once you have incorporated and have your business set up, you can apply for your own liability insurance.

CROSSING THE BRIDGE

STUDIO SEVEN
Healthy Inspired Action

Step Seven: Be a Business Information Gateway

Track Balanced Action combined with Appreciation
and Gratitude will Magnetize Inspiration and Success

CHAPTER TWENTY-FOUR

Discipline the Fun Way

"I've learned that you can't have everything and do everything at the same time." —Oprah Winfrey

Get in the habit of serving the world with gratitude, appreciation and kindness from your heart. This is how you make the world a better place and further your inspiration.

Another way to increase your value and worth is to always do your best work and only show your best work in all you do. When you cooperate in your own success, as well as the success of others around you, there is now a fun journey of co-creation and co-operation that happens. Focus on making decisions that lead you to your future and that serve the highest good of others with your knowledge. We live in an abundant Universe and everything you do is part of that divine perfection and unlimited power to create. This flows through you and everyone. The keys in this studio toolbox are Discipline and Perseverance and will inspire and promote your radiant success.

The price of success is discipline. The discipline may not necessarily be the type you think it is. Your ego, or inner critic, may pop in and say you're still not good enough; it may say that you need more education, another book or class. Do not fall for it! Make a habit of noticing what unsuccessful artists hate to do. "You know what I hate to do?" they say; you can hear the complaints all around you. "I hate to sell…I hate to talk about my art." The unsuccessful would prefer to stay stuck, taking 40 years of classes on how to make art rather than actually make and sell art. They come to me all the time and ask, "Do you teach art?" When I reply, "I teach you how to sell art. You are already a master at making art. I teach you to take your knowledge, apply it, and make a business of it so you can support yourself doing what you love to do. Would you like to sell your art?" Guess what happens when I ask that question most of the time? They run! Scared, they continue to choose to stay stuck in the fear of not being a good enough artist. Art students that I have spoken with believe that the galleries are going to call them when they finish school. Guess what? They're not and they don't care. Why? They don't know the artists exist.

Choose to do the opposite of those stuck and waiting artists. It's time to wake up and take action using your knowledge. Listen to what the other artists hate doing and make what you love doing, your art, from your heart, the best that you know how to. Tell people about it or else no one will know who you are! Tell your Art to Sell your Art!

In the meantime, keep improving your skills and personal style. If you don't practice your craft for a week, you notice. If you don't practice your craft for a month, your associates notice. If you don't practice your craft for a year, your customers notice. Keep that up and you'll be miserable and most likely out of business.

Visualize to Real-ize

Use any of the exercises in this book and visualize to 'REAL'-ize. You do it naturally anyway whether it's a good thing or a bad thing. Knowing enough or not knowing enough, go for it anyway and see the good in all of it and what it can teach you. Begin now to discipline yourself to serve the world with gratitude, appreciation and kindness from your heart in doing what you love to. By thinking and focusing on your vision of what you love to do, create a vibration that calls on inspiration and creativity from your higher source, not your ego. First, you create through vibration of thought and then comes the physical part, action!

Artists, writers, actors, musicians and athletes call it being in the zone. I'm not talking of tedious work here, that's your ego. It's very easy to become busy 'being busy,' something you don't want. Remember, balance is the key here, so keep taking action to avoid getting lost and sidetracked from your vision. When in action, re-group daily by focusing and holding onto your vision, trusting the process and continuing to take more action.

Like planting seeds, this all takes nurturing and patience. So, tend to your soil, your foundations, give them the ideal growing conditions and trust that the seeds will sprout. The ship will come in, but first it must be built and then launched. Remember?

If you're an artist, you can't expect to get a show or exhibition without any of your own art. The same goes for the rest of us. In order to get the seed to grow, you have to prepare the soil.

Let Go and Let God

Unless you turn over to your higher self, source, spirit, God force, whatever you believe in, nothing will happen. Perhaps this is why so many people say, "Let Go and Let God". Many people mistranslate that as, "let it go and be apathetic." Don't do this; that's not what it means at all. Release your tight hold! Build your ship well, do your work and then let it go out to do what it was meant to do.

My friend, artist Bonnie Druschel, shared her story of taking healthy inspired action.

"Years ago when I wanted to license my artwork, I wrote down on a piece of paper 12 times "my artwork is licensed world-wide." My handwriting was messy and I kept making mistakes all the time. However, eventually after doing it over and over again...I began to believe it and my handwriting improved and at my first tradeshow at the Javits Center in NYC, I landed my first licensing contract and my artwork was produced on mugs, magnets, gift-bags, journals and a line of brooches as well sold in the U.S. and Canada. I learned about the writing 12 times per day from Scott Adams' "Dilbert" cartoon. This is what he did to land his first syndicated cartoon."

It worked for Bonnie and it may work for you. I do a similar exercise with artists who come to me for advice. When artists come to me asking for representation, or how to get a gallery show, I ask him/her a few questions about discipline, consistency and the quality of their portfolio. I usually give them a little exercise. I advise them to have a body of work, consisting of their absolute best work, to show a gallery. Many artists have come back to thank me.

You can see Bonnie's beautiful inspiring art here http://www.bonniedruschel.com/

As an artist, you want to know yourself deep down inside that it is your absolute best. Don't you agree? The way I like to do this is to make 20 different pieces of art in the same theme or subject. Both work well. You can do this as well.

20 Times Best in Show

This exercise is called "20 times Best In Show." It is a powerful way to create and show your best work. If you're a visual artist this takes time and you won't be able do it all at once, so don't even try.

1. You begin by making 20 small pieces of art, say drawings on pads no larger than 11 x 14 inches in size. Out of those 20 pieces of art you create, select ONE, the very best piece out of the group of 20; set it aside. This is your perfect piece, your best in show.
2. Now, take those 19 other art pieces and put them away. Repeat the process again nineteen times, and again pick the best from the twenty.
3. When you're finished with this process, you will have 20 pieces of your best work for your exhibit and 380 drawings for your portfolio.

Perhaps you will toss some of them, but you now have an extensive collection of drawings. Now you know why it is important to work small here, because besides time consumption, the art will take up space. When you present these 20 pieces to a customer, gallery owner, or anyone who asks to see your portfolio, you will know deep in your heart that this is your very best work. The good energy vibration from your portfolio will be picked up by the person you are showing your work to. They, in turn, will know that this is a Big Picture of your very best work! Will you get the job? Would you get the show? That is to be determined, but you have learned a great lesson in persistence and discipline doing the thing you love, knowing deep inside that you have expressed and shown your very best work and that you are a professional.

Creating what you love to create is a form of meditation that artists benefit from like no one else. Enjoy it! Get in the zone and do it, release the outcome to the Universe, but keep creating and nurturing your garden! Creativity flows through us, not from us. Practicing this will open up your channel, tapping into the unlimited power source where all brilliance comes from. Are you getting The Big Picture?

An Example of 20 Times

Here is my story with 20 times Best In Show. I had always wanted to be in an art book with other artists and since I was a little child, I had visualized that someday this would happen. When I was living in Los Angeles and my art career was just starting to blossom locally, I received a fax at home. My roommate, Gary, ran into the kitchen hollering with joy, "Oh, my! Oh, my!" Seemingly out of nowhere was a faxed letter from a London art historian and publisher, Aubrey Walter. The letter stated that he had a postcard above his computer with my art on it and that he had been looking at it for the last year. Mr. Walter was in the process of compiling a book of American artists and he inquired whether I had other samples of my work to share with him. He mentioned that the picture of my painting on the postcard was one of his favorites and had brought him joy every time he saw it. Mr. Walter wanted me to be a part of his next art book project. He needed at least 20 slides of my best work delivered to him within one week. While my jaw dropped, Gary was ecstatic; he was leaving for London the next day to visit a friend. Did I ever pay attention! Woo-hoo!

You see, a few months prior, I had spoken with an artist friend who had achieved good success in getting gallery shows in the area. He advised me always to have a show of my best work ready to hang. He said it should always be at least 20 pieces. So, I thought to myself, why not have three or four shows ready to go? I had some time on my hands, so I created a large body of work and photographed it in slides, before the digital image age. Without realizing it, I had created a Big Picture of all of my very best work. I already had them labeled and into presentation sheets. All I had to do was put them in an envelope and send them to Mr. Walter! I decided to send about 80 slides just in case. Gary, who left for England the very next day, delivered them to Mr. Walter's office forty-eight hours later. Talk about being grateful! Being in the right place at the right time allowed everything to flow perfectly. Within a couple days I received a fax from England stating, "My goodness! Your work is beautiful! I believe you deserve your very own book. What do you think?" Well, I can tell you what I thought and by two years later I had a book about my art internationally published and sold on four different continents. Life can change at any moment when you are prepared and in the mindset to accept it.

The Personal Touch

While people may find you in many different ways, such as finding my postcard on the Internet, there is nothing like the personal touch in the art business. Since the Internet phenomenon began, art sales have steadily increased in my own business. Having said that, they account for less than 10 % of my annual sales. I am grateful for those customers, however, if I depended only on my Internet presence, I would be missing out on more than 90 percent of my income! Counting on a possible customer/collector to buy from your website alone without your assistance is one of the quickest ways to lose a sale, especially when they are in your physical presence and you send them there (or you think you do).

While it's important to have a website, sending a future client to the Internet is usually the weakest way for an artist to give a presentation. If the art collector goes there at all, they don't get the magical experience of seeing a live, interactive dialogue exchanged between the art and the artist.

Having direct contact with the art, and when possible, the artist who created it, will give your client maximum opportunity to fall in love with and want your creation. If you plan on selling your art to clients through an online presence, show them how to navigate your site and give them useful information. Consider personally walking them through the website so you can sell your art while you're both on the site together. If they are a collector of your work, you may have to do this more than once or even every time. Is this how you want to sell your work or just an aspect of it? You get to decide.

Learn to be aware of your surroundings and attitudes. In previous relaxation and replenishing exercises, you learned to fine tune your awareness; we are like magnets and sponges, so pay attention to what's going on around you. As you attract what you want, that synchronistic energy begins to attract more and more and like compound interest; whatever you put in comes back to you multiplied. When we pay attention and come from integrity, we can embrace healthy challenges and applaud other's successes. Everything is right on time, never too late, and now you are taking action on your dreams.

You are the source responsible for your abundance. Believe in yourself confidently and lovingly, knowing that you are love, are loving and lovable. Create goals that are clear and create supportive disciplinary habits that take your knowledge and artistic license to new levels. Having clear goals for yourself is an act of self-love. When your goals are clear, you can move in positive ways toward your desires and your ultimate future. By doing this, you will create joy and confidence. When you know what your passions and heart's desires are, you can make decisions that will improve your life greatly. Now, get into action with discipline and perseverance!

Chapter Twenty-Four's Studio Play Sheet

Be part of the Big Picture. Visit museums and galleries. See if your ego or inner critic pops in while looking around. If so, learn to gently smile and lovingly laugh at it, to help loosen you up. Look for the divine brilliance in the art around you. Was there something similar or something you can relate to that the artist tapped into?

Listen to classical music and see if you have any similar experiences.

Dance, take yoga and do anything that loosens you up physically.

If your funds were unlimited and you could do it all the time, what is it that you would love to do or create?

Whatever it is that you love to create, focus on it and create it 20 times Best In Show. This practice of doing your best work always allows you to see yourself as the source of your abundance, builds confidence and helps you enjoy the process of getting there as much as the goal. 20 Times Best In Show prepares you to be ready immediately and move forward when opportunity knocks.

Think about it and create a loving vibration about what you love to do; then, practice and do that thing first in your mind and then for real, 20 times Best In Show. Whether you're doing a presentation, writing a speech, making an art piece, making music, playing sports, or whatever it is that you do, shine light on your craft and talents and bring them into the light. Once again, get in the habit of serving the world with gratitude, appreciation, artistic discipline and kindness from your heart; this is how you make the world a better place.

Creative Activity Points

Tell your Art to Sell your Art.

Always have an appointment before going into a gallery.

Do not be an undercover artist acting like a customer then pouncing on galleries staff with your portfolio on cell phone device, I-pad, notebook etc. You won't score points.

Get a real portfolio.

Being on exhibit or adding another line to your resume is not the reason to be in a gallery. The reason to be there is to sell your art and make a living.

Artists who do not want to sell their original work yet who still want to make a living with their art, should create shows or exhibits that feature their print work for sale.

Create art shows and exhibits with an admission fee that benefits a favorite charity.

In gallery sales, the most important person to you as the artist is not the customer; it is the salesperson or sales team manager, who in turn, makes the customer the most important.

Do not sell or market your art while in a bad mood.

Thank people before they buy something. For example: Hello welcome to my art show, thank you for taking time to look at my work.

We see things in pictures and pictures sell. During conversation, place a picture with your words into your prospect customers mind. Such as, "Where do you see this in your home?" Or "Where or when will you have me singing my songs or signing my book at your party?"

Conflicting stories create confusion. Tell the truth in your stories. Be sure your sales team does so as well.

Once you tell your story to sell your art, let it go and act as if you don't need the sale. A confident artist trumps a desperate artist every time.

Play 20 Times Best In Show to practice and improve your craft.

Create a Negotiation Checklist, with things you will consider and things you won't. From the things you will consider negotiating, create a plan.

You don't have to sell your art to a buyer; you could rent it, license it or loan it for fees over and over again. Think outside the box.

When selling, exhibiting or renting, have clear agreements including written contracts which include: sale price, payment, delivery, risk of loss, liability insurance, copyright, reproduction and ownership to heirs and successors.

When selling through a gallery, have a clear and signed agreement that states that discounting your art comes out of the gallery's commission, not yours.

At times, customers may contact you stating that they've been to the gallery and that they attempt to go around the gallery for a better price. Never send a message to the public that they can go around your business partners. Why be in a gallery in the first place if you do this? Explain that you are contracted with the gallery. Have the gallery contact them or send them back to the gallery for a deal, not through you. The gallery can negotiate on their side of their commission, not yours.

If you have a website with your art prices posted on it, they should reflect and be consistent with the prices that are at your gallery space as well.

Always make people happy to hear from you by giving them useful information that they can use rather than giving them a sales pitch every time they see your art.

When a potential customer is in your presence and asks if you have a website, get to the point and find out if they are serious or not, instead of handing them marketing items that cost you money right away. Say, "Yes, let me show you how to navigate the site," and walk them over to a computer, show them on a phone device, get their email, and sign them up for a newsletter. If they are not interested, they will make another excuse. Let them go, for if they are really interested, you will have developed your customer service better because you have shown interest in them.

Make postcards of your art with contact information on both sides, such as your website. Do this on business cards as well.

Give two postcards to everyone you talk to about your art, one for them and one for their friend who loves art. Ask if they need more than two.

On postcards, business cards, brochures and any printed material the goes out to promote your business product, blog, video or website put a Q.R.CODE (quick response) code on your material. This is a marketing tool for owners of devices with smart phones technology to find your product by taking a picture of your promotional material. Every time you use a QR code, be sure the URL, website it takes the potential customer to is printed below the QR code for people who do not have smart phone technology. This makes it easy for everyone to find your product, page or info.

Create a video for you're the top of your web page, blog and also post it to YouTube and drive traffic to your sites.

CHAPTER TWENTY FIVE

Contribute Support with Your Highest Level of Permission

"If we all did the things we are capable of doing, we would literally astound ourselves." —Thomas A. Edison

I have met my friend Rayme Sciaroni 'accidentally' many times at coffee over the years. Rayme is a multi-talented artist who has got his creative fingers in several different areas in life: composing, writing, crafting, directing and designing. He also has his own web-cast radio show followed by fans in over one hundred countries. The Universe seems to pair us up once in a while when we are both needing and desiring to share and inspire each other.

On one recent morning, my brilliant friend was telling me how he is getting ready to direct a very large and expensive production of 'Beauty and the Beast.' Knowing the obvious pit-falls that come from doing an already very well-known musical, his desire to keep it fresh and alive and stand out from other productions is vital to him. His first couple of production meetings, including a pre-audition meeting with potential cast members, lead him to a very simple, yet fresh and joyful approach for what he is looking to achieve.

Working first with the stage designer, costume designer and hair/make-up artist, they first bantered about ideas and he realized what he had to do. "Give them permission to create at their highest level. I saw them start out a bit timidly when they showed me what their biggest vision of the show would be." After realizing this, Rayme said, "Go ahead and create the biggest and grandest vision of what you'd like to see and then we'll take it from there."

Rayme continued to tell me, "The instant look of joy and inspiration that these people took from that statement was probably a bigger lesson for me. I just gave them permission to be their grandest, most creative selves! And isn't that what we all want anyway? So, when I went to talk to the pre-audition people, they wanted to know what I would be looking for at the auditions. And I said to them, "I am looking to create a larger, more joyful, sparkly production. So please come to me and bring your absolute best, biggest and brightest self. I am finding this to be quite powerful and I know that I will continuously remind myself to ALWAYS BE at my biggest, brightest, best self every minute of every day. It's where we ALL truly live anyway." Learn more about Rayme at www.raymecards.com and www.raymemusic.com .

Mastermind Groups

Create a supportive, objective, insightful, and mentoring mastermind team for your art business, no matter what capacity or level you take your business. This will enhance and ignite your Big Picture. Research how to form a mastermind group, as there are rules to follow when you are in session. The good book says, "Wherever two or more are gathered…" Take this seriously. All you need is one other person to start and probably a maximum of six persons. Any more than that and it takes too much time. You can have more than one group, as well, for the different areas of your life that you want to expand upon. Start with one area and take it from there. This is an accountability group. Like a board of directors, you will be there to nurture each other professionally as role models by offering suggestions and seeking advice, reporting on progress and submitting new ideas for success while holding one another accountable. Each person gets equal amounts of time to speak, offer assistance and inquire about situations in which they need insight. These group meetings are confidential and include team building exercises. Like Rayme, give your group full permission to express their highest creative selves.

Seek out supportive persons from different walks of life, backgrounds, and occupations, who compliment your passions and desires for your mastermind team. It is important to associate with people who believe in what you are doing, will hold you accountable and reinforce new modes of behavior for your success and vice versa, both in and out of the meeting environment.

Create mastermind groups for unstoppable success and amazing friendships. Do NOT get a group of people that will say yes to your every whim. This group should challenge you and suggest new ways of looking at things professionally. If you need a group of yes-people, this is not the venue. You are seeking support from people who know answers that you do not. They have reaped success in area you wish to more about and you all support each other with your expertise and suggestions.

Turn a Problem into Gold

Can you turn one of your problems into a service that reaps financial success? When I was looking at getting into local galleries, no one wanted to exhibit my art. Every art competition I participated in gladly took my entry fee but declined me. I realized that art fairs and many competitions were ridiculous ego trips for the artist and a way to raise quick cash for associations and promotion companies who knew nothing of art, yet charged high entrance fees, promising thousands of visitors. *What type of visitors?* I wondered. *Did they have sales numbers to back up their entry fee?* These are good questions to consider. I had no interest in being associated with these gimmicky charades.

After number crunching, I realized that having my own gallery and art publishing company was more cost effective in the long run. I made a decision to put myself in charge of my art career and financially reaped the benefits of doing so. I put together my dream team of experts, did my research, shared it with other artists and before I knew it, people in the area were calling me The California Artist! A gallery located in one of America's most visited state parks, I did my homework and became responsible for my art career. Other folks came along and when they wanted to help, I let them run with it. We all grew together.

Take charge of your problems and look for the biggest, most wild solutions. Problems most often hold the answers to your passion and financial success. Sometimes the most irritating and frustrating problems can lead you to your biggest freedom. You might not be able to see the solution, but another creative person may offer you a bigger, bolder solution than you could have ever thought of. Give yourself permission to be open to co-creative support.

Are you just starting out or getting back on track in the artist business? It takes more than just some capitol it takes creativity, organization and perseverance. It also takes training yourself then training others to do your job. Here's a good two-part process to follow:

Part One:

1. Make a close connection with businesspersons who know what they are talking about, interview them and follow their lead. Success in business over 5 years old is a good indicator.
2. Put a specific amount of time (and time of day) aside to study more about what you want to learn in that field. A half hour a day and at the same time of day is good.
3. See if the numbers work for you. If the numbers add up, go for it. If the numbers don't add up in your favor, then there is a step missing somewhere. Don't get into business unless the numbers work in your favor!
4. Give co-creators (people you are working with, assisting you and for you) permission to create at their highest level.
5. Do not worry or care about what other people think about your stuff. This is the recipe for no regrets. Just get to work on your dream!

Part Two

1. Get good leads for your art sales. Let bad ones go.
2. Know what to say to those leads in person or via correspondence.
3. Train people to do the first two steps.
4. Commit to doing the first three steps and AGAIN give people permission to be creative at their highest level; that's how you grow your art business.

No matter what happened yesterday, today is a new day and you can work wonders with that. It's time to rise and shine; act with love and gratitude.

Never discuss your failures with artists less successful than you, including your sales partners and staff. They will love to mentor you on continued similar circumstances and how to do what they don't do. Seek advice from those who have been there and who have real insight. Seek a mentor; be a mentor.

Just like making your art, on the business side of it, the more you explore and the more energy you put into it, the more you will get out of it.

Chapter Twenty-Five's Studio Play Sheet

What types of persons would be great for your mastermind dream team to success?

What types of questions do you need to ask your mastermind dream team to grow your heart's desires, your business, investment or travel plans?

What would you name your mastermind dream team?

What type of teaching program could you create to share your art that leads to more business?

What is biggest and grandest vision of what you'd like to see?

Ask others what is their biggest and grandest vision of what they would like to see for their Big Picture too.

Creative Activity Points

Seek business advice from business owners who are more successful than you.

Seek advice from those who have been there and those who have real insight.

Seek a business mentor; be a business mentor.

Professional advice should be sought from a person in the field in which you are seeking knowledge. If there are no experts in that field, become one. Become an expert in your field and then teach it to others.

If the numbers don't add up, the numbers don't add up! Positive cash flow means a profit.

Participate in art competitions or art fairs where your fees support the local community in a beneficial way. It will be stated right up front when they do.

Never pay to be in a gallery unless you own it and are paying the lease, rent or mortgage.

Set time aside everyday to study something new that you can apply to your business art career.

CHAPTER TWENTY-SIX

Goal Setting

"Nothing can stop the man with the right mental attitude from achieving his goal; nothing on earth can help the man with the wrong mental attitude." —Thomas Jefferson

If you want to make a living with your art, YOU MUST HAVE GOALS.
Just like you did with your Heart's Art Desire exercise, you can and should turn your affirmations into concrete goals. Then, turn your goals into real manifestations. Do this by acting as if you already have achieved your goals. By acting AS IF it is like you are charging a battery deep within you. This keeps you energized with more and more positive power, magnetizing more synchronicity to you. Create personal and impersonal goals from your affirmations. You will not reach any positive goals without a clear and believable plan.

Pursue at least one impersonal goal. An impersonal goal is one that betters another more than you. By doing this, you often discover a purpose greater than yourself. When you are willing to do this the rewards can be tremendous, including feeling good inside! Start with a local charity close to your heart. So many people need your wisdom, inspiration and help in general. Impersonal goals are more about the impact on other people than on you. Could you volunteer or speak to a group? Could you help a neighbor?

How you get to your goals is also very important. What if you are planning a trip to a place that you had never been? Suppose you purchased a new application or roadmap to get there. Would you use your new tools to get where you wanted to go? Would you look at them? Or would you just go off in any direction? Your intuition is like a roadmap; how you develop your mind to use it is up to you. In order to achieve you goals, you must clearly know what they are and create a plan to follow through on all aspects of it. Artists who succeed always know where they are going, even if they can't see the end result physically. Life is too short to judge your future based on the past.

One more thing on goals and success is that success is a result. It most often occurs quietly and privately. Success is not a goal; it is an occurrence resulting *from* a goal or many goals coming to fruition. It's a state of mind and being. Just by being alive, you are a success!

Chapter Twenty-Six's Studio Play Sheet

Make a Big Picture Roadmap
What is your goal?

1. Describe the goal explicitly and concisely.
2. Give your goal a deadline (when you will arrive) and make a promise to yourself to get there. Sign and date it.
3. Identify potential obstacles on the way.

Be prepared to turn them into opportunity. Do your research on your goal.

4. List the skills you have or need to acquire to get to the goal destination.
5. List helpful people, resources and experts that will help you achieve this goal.
6. List the benefits you will receive from achieving this goal.
7. Develop a workable plan that gets you there.

If you want to achieve your goal in seven years, count backwards. What has to happen seven, six, five, four, three, two, one year(s) from now? Six months, three months, two months, one month, two weeks, one week, tomorrow, today? Do that now.

8. Be accountable to yourself and have others hold you accountable.

Make a list of the people that you will ask to hold you accountable. Now, contact them.

9. List the action things you are going to do in order to get you to your goal.

(This is your road map.)

Creative Activity Points

Identify one impersonal goal a month that helps another, something from the heart, perhaps helping an elderly neighbor with a chore, it could be a simple as sweeping their walkway. Perhaps purchasing some extra products like tooth brush and toothpaste and just handing it to a person in need on the street. Drop off a bag of groceries at a local shelter or recovery home. No one knows about except you. Keep it to yourself; it's a secret. You could be someone's angel.

You will be more successful at making a living with your art when you stop defending what you think you know.

Develop an insatiable need to know more about how to deliver your product. Then take what you learn and do it.

Have clear goals.

Write out a precise believable plan with descriptions of the way you will reach the achievement of your goals.

Long-term goals are a must because they keep you on your toes and keep you from getting too lazy, frustrated or comfortable.

Be sure that your goals are concrete and of substance in order to manifest them into reality.

When you reach your goal, celebrate it and record it. Write down what you achieved and date it.

Stretch and expand your goals; make them bigger so that you do not get stuck.

CHAPTER TWENTY-SEVEN

Keep Track of Your Successes

"When you focus on new goals, you give your mind a new set of eyes to see new things, circumstances, situations, and persons and so forth to focus on and that's how your dreams begin to get accomplished." —RD Riccoboni

Let's talk about more ways of turning negative thoughts and fears, because they pop in when you least expect it. The best line of defense for continued growth and success is this. Focus on and Keep Track of the Good Stuff.

We live in a world of duality: good stuff and bad stuff. Start by looking for those things that always work out for the best and start keeping track of them. You will start seeing those things, the evidence, that is around you at all times. Your energy attracts things by virtue of what you pay attention to and focus upon.

The more you focus on the good stuff, the less powerful and prevalent the bad stuff becomes. When bad stuff happens, turn it around and ask yourself, "What is the good in this situation?"

There is great power in either one, so which do you want to give the greater power to? Which thing do you want to give less of your power to? Here's a big secret; to avoid becoming lost or sidetracked, continue to focus on your vision while you're taking action. Keep your vision index card nearby and review it often.

Just because you can keep score doesn't mean you should. You can journal your experience of victimization every morning and that will only perpetuate your sense of oppression and keep you stuck. Why not keep score of the good stuff?! *Your* good stuff. Unless you are paid or elected to do so, keep score of your own success only. You are not in the business of judging others.

Just because you can compete doesn't mean you should. Compete with yourself by stretching and expanding your goals. Remember the Big Picture is yours!

When making a bold move, use common sense. Do you react or respond? A well thought-out responsible move goes farther than a reactionary move.

Keep dated records of the achievements you attract and steps you wish to repeat. They'll inspire and save you time going forward. Keep a journal by the side of your bed and make dated one-line entries. Try it. It's a fun record to look back on and helps develop confidence, gratitude and appreciation for your achievements, accomplishments. And, it's all-around great evidence of your journey to success. Good record keeping is essential as you make a living as an artist.

Take photos of your magnificent artist life; illustrate your journal with them.

I keep a positive-evidence journal on my nightstand by the side of my bed. When something wonderful happens, I write it down. When I am feeling distracted, I reflect and read my positive evidence and all the wonderful things I have attracted and that I am grateful for. This type of journal records your success story. I highly recommend keeping one. You can see an example of mine on my website and order one like the one I use or create your own. Mine is called "My Magnificent Evidence Journal" and the cover illustrates one of my paintings of a big sailing ship at sunrise.

The one I've designed and illustrated includes some of my favorite affirmations and sketches. Order My Magnificent Evidence Journal", or "My Positive Evidence Journal" on my website http://rdriccoboni.com or make your own.

Chapter Twenty-Seven's Studio Play Sheet

Make a "Magnificent Evidence" Journal

Get a spiral notebook and keep a dated record of all your positive and magnificent evidence; write neatly so that you can review it later on.

Directions:

On the first page, write an inscription to yourself promising that you will only enter positive, uplifting, insightful and wonderful things that happen to you on your journey.

Then, sign and date it and begin focusing on the "good stuff".

Creative Activity Points

Who did you meet that helped your success today?

Send them a thank you card with your business card attached.

Take photos with your clients, friends and associates. Artists usually hang out with an awesome group of people. Post them up and share; those people love you.

Keep a good record of your success, both financial and non-financial.

Keep all business records safe and secure in a responsible filing system that is easily accessible.

Back up computer files both internally and externally off your computer.

More than one external back up place is good.

Be sure to update your external back up files on a regular basis.

CHAPTER TWENTY-EIGHT

Invest in Your Talent to Find Your Calling

"Don't aim for success if you want it; just do what you love and believe in, and it will come naturally."—David Frost

How do you invest in yourself become a successful artist?

You must invest and trust in yourself first before anyone else will. The level at which you invest in yourself becomes the level at which others will invest in you. Are you worth others investing in your art for? You must believe you are! When you are answering your calling, you are on the right track.

Investing can be done in different ways. One major way to invest is when you pay for knowledge (such as classes to expand your talents), which many times is necessary to learn how things work out there in the real world. However, knowledge is completely useless if you do not apply what you have learned. The other way of learning is through life experiences. They both can cost you monetarily and emotionally. This is why it is important to take notice of what it is that you really like to do and where your interest is guiding you. Just because some other artist, teacher or businessperson (including myself) says you should do it this way or that way doesn't mean it is the right path right for you.

My Talent Is Not My Calling

I learned this myself and my talent alone is not my calling. I have much more fun inspiring others than actually painting a picture. I love making my art, tapping into source energy when I do it and seeing how people react and get inspired when they view it. But, my talent is one of the tools I use along the way to discovering my calling and it is necessary that I manually get into action to create the work that moves me along my path. I just don't like to get distracted from my own personal path. Here's an example:

The Law of Attraction vs. A Side Show Attraction

I have been asked to paint in public at galleries, events and even in my place of business. I don't mind painting in front of people; in fact, when friends visit me at my home and I am working on a painting, I love to chat with them while I'm working on the piece. Doing this in a place of business attracts a very different outcome and chaotic energy. In a place of business, this activity creates theater. When you go to the theater, do you pay for the performance before you see it or after? When you don't pay for a performance, what is it? It's an attraction or an amenity for something else.

Here is where knowing what you want will pay off. What type of income do you want to generate with your art? If you want to be an attraction or an amenity, be sure that you are paid beforehand; otherwise, just like when you go to the movies, the concert or the play, when the show is over and you put down your paint brush, everyone leaves and you left all alone to clean up your stage.

Should you decide to paint publicly, you may want to create a good buzz, get people into a bidding war against each other and sell your painting to the highest bidder, perhaps benefitting a local charity. You can sell the finished painting to both the highest bidder and the runner up by creating a similar painting for the second highest bidder. I like to call this Sold! And Sold! That's right! You just sold two paintings and one has not yet been painted!

Note: If you are not in a gallery setting when you do this, be sure you are in compliance with local laws; have business permits on the streets and make sure you are able to take immediate payment for the work should you decide to do something like this. If you are a vendor at an art fair, a permit is usually covered through the promoter but a temporary permit may still be needed in some cities.

Now do not get me wrong. It is fascinating to see the artist create live, demonstrating their techniques at the gallery where you can ask them questions and see a painting unfold before your eyes. But, being a side show is not my calling and I leave this to the ones who want to do this sort of performance art. It takes a tremendous amount of energy, organization and assistance to do it correctly. The same applies to craft and art fairs. I realized it was less costly to have a permanent roof over art instead of schlepping art all around the country to art events. Some artists love doing the art fair circuit and painting at live events, however most artists I have spoken with do not. We artists all seem to have to try a bit of everything until we find what works best for us individually. Before you are asked to do an exhausting event and say yes or no, learn how to think through what is within your means and how you will be compensated. Then, be firm in your decision.

You are an Investment Too

The artist and the art created are both investments. People automatically assume many false things about artists; being great at business is not one of them. Prove them wrong. Sometimes people do not think or respect art or artists. They ask for freebies and can do silly, uninteded things that put the art in jeopardy, like pointing at the art with an umbrella on a rainy day, or setting a drink on top of a piece of art while looking at another piece. Sometimes, people just don't think through what could happen if something slips or falls. Other times, people are just plain rude, running into a gallery to take a cell phone call because it's quiet, or walking right up to an art piece without permission and taking detailed photographs of it. And, even when told not to do that, they try and take one or two more. My all-time brainless favorite people are those who walk into the gallery with food in tow, pointing at art work with an oversized lopsided ice cream cone. Yes, people will be atrocious and walk into an art gallery, vendor booth or exclusive country club show and do all these things. Let them have it, with class at first; be firm and stand up for yourself and the art. Be clear as soon as they approach your art and put it in some sort of peril. You can have all the warning signs in the world posted around your work but nothing works better than speaking up for yourself.

When you have to be firm, be kind and tell it like it is. You may be perceived as a bitch, but you don't have to be an ass. Frankly, who cares when these people don't respect you, your art or your place of business? Do not send mixed signals or be wishy-washy in business. When you do such things, it's just dishonest to all including yourself. If you have staff, co-worker artists and even previous customers and collectors who look up to you, being inconsistent is telling them that it's okay not to respect you or your art. When you do this it's, "good bye business!"

Standing up for yourself and don't being distracted from your Big Picture. That is investing in yourself. It will build confidence.

Other Ways to Invest

Another way you can invest in you is by being a part of someone else's art project from beginning to end, such as doing volunteer work or taking on a part time job in areas you need to build up knowledge and strength in. Learning the ropes by assisting others helps create a new point of view, new learned steps and brand of artistry that you can later apply to your own craft. I learned how to make an art show look good from working with many non-profit fundraisers and art organizations over the years.

The only way to make your career financially bloom through your investments is to do the work required by getting on board with action somewhere with others. Your knowledge without work will do nothing to make things materialize.

Where can your previous life experiences help you now? Those life experiences are investments and it is a given that all of them may not have been good. Do not dwell on failures of the past. There are many happenings that were great when you look back at them.

Some of my valuable personal investments where from past jobs that had nothing to do with my art, but what I learned there has everything to do with making a living from it today. In banking, I learned how to balance my checkbook as well as how to have valuable customer service, retail selling and organization skills. In Human Resources, I learned valuable people skills and how to deal with difficult situations when creating and marketing fun events. And, managing a retail store and shop-keeping incorporated aspects of all the jobs. I learned to further carry my weight responsibly and that my behavior affected the bottom line no matter what. I learned to pay attention and listen for what the customer was actually asking for and how to anticipate objections by asking provocative questions about how to make *their* dreams come true, not mine. I learned how to illustrate how my services could help them accomplish that.

We are all gifted and talented. But what is your calling? Ask yourself where and what is your calling? Talent is not your calling. Talent is the tool for tapping into and investing in your calling. Your calling is where you reap the benefits of having done the artwork; it is where your authentic artist self plays and grows.

Use all the previous exercises in this book to achieve the things you want; modify them to your personal artist living practices. Remember, your subconscious mind cannot tell the difference between what's real and what's imagined!

The majority of an artist's money-making problem is mostly mental in nature and based on old, limited beliefs from which there are no solutions. Limited beliefs are usually false, and when dwelled on long enough, they manifest into reality. Choose good beliefs with repetition!

Earlier we went over switching statements to rid yourself of those old, incorrect beliefs, replace your views of why you can't do something into views of why you CAN. Keep that up when negative thoughts and issues pop up. Write down what you have wanted to do that is legal and safe and the reasons why you believe you can't do that. Refer to the Studio Sheets in Chapter Two for a more in-depth review.

Now, write the reasons WHY YOU CAN do it. Get it out of your head and onto the paper. This is how an artist creates a work of art; and a business solution not to mention a picture of a successful life. Be a master artist for your life and create a phenomenal learning exercise for yourself. Step up to the canvas of your life.

No one really knows what our minds are capable of. Look at the many things thought up, invented and created since you were a child. Or better yet, look at all that has been created that has made the world a better place since your great grandparents were children. Use your brilliant mind and switch it from what you can't do to what you can. You are a master artist.

Master your mind and emotions; change your thinking and start thinking the right way. Write down why you can do something and notice how positive it feels inside.

Master your time. Once the moment is gone, never look back. Master the time you get, which is right now. Get into action and stay on top of your artistic heart's desires and passions. Too much action and you will be overwhelmed; you'll know it. Some things you will need to drop, so prioritize your projects and ask for help! Pay someone to do certain tasks. When you get help, don't micro-manage; let your helper run with it. If they need help, don't hire another person; suggest they get help as well. Create a new economy for yourself and others. Become an art-preneur.

Master your communication. Listen first, and then ask questions to make sure you heard correctly. Make decisions and choices that are appropriate for your desired outcome.

Master both appreciation and gratitude. Be thankful for 'it' before 'it' even arrives.

Again, think of holding a puppy or kitten and the feeling that it gives you. Be a resource to those who request your help.

Master what you want and practice scenarios that feel good. You've got to want your goal passionately. You've got to want success and live by it. Now, go get to it!

As you begin to shine, more and more talent people will be drawn to you.

You may want to explore new ventures that get you closer to your calling.

Chapter Twenty-Eight's Studio Play Sheet

Choose five things that are legal and safe that you think you cannot do.

1.

2.

3.

4.

5.

Now, write down (for each) more than five reasons why you can do them. Don't stop until you have at least five reasons why you can do these things.

I can accomplish number one because…..

1.

2.

3.

4.

5.

I can accomplish number two because…..

1.

2.

3.

4.

5.

I can accomplish number three because…..

1.

2.

3.

4.

5.

I can accomplish number four because…..

1.

2.

3.

4.

5.

I can accomplish number five because…..

1.

2.

3.

4.

5.

Why would you invest your energy in something that you dislike? Your time is valuable, so don't look back on those five things that you think you cannot do ever again. You now have over 25 reasons why you *can* do the things. It is time to take a risk and start asking the right questions of others; listen for the answers that can help aid you in accomplishing these things.

Creative Activity Points

Make a list and keep track of the people who helped you accomplish these things so that you can appreciate with gratitude those people who helped you along the way. Call them, write them and thank them and tell them what you're up to.

Having too many projects at once can be overwhelming. You can't do everything; let others help you so you can prioritize and focus on what you are best at.

We all have expertise in different areas. Expand your economy wisely by being of service and creating service in areas of life that you love and adore. Invest in yourself.

Correctly copyright your work. Consult the copyright office and/or an intellectual property attorney. Be smart; protect your investment. Most of the information that artists pass around is hearsay, such as mailing pictures of your art to yourself in a sealed envelope. Nice try; don't do that. Protect your work the right way.

Consider making a professionally manufactured book, catalog or portfolio of your artwork. A perfect bound or hardcover book can be made on many on-demand self-publishing sites. Upload pictures of your art directly to their templates, follow their directions and tips and then create your art portfolio book. You can order one, or many, on-demand. Prices vary greatly so again, do your homework before you invest your time and money.

Consider registering you entire collection of art that you created in your portfolio book under one copyright saving you lots of time and money.

You can give these portfolio books away on occasion and best of all, you can pre-sell them and order more! Now you have a product. Invest in yourself!

Pay yourself first. If you don't get paid, no one else does either. Think about that.

Consider hiring a consultant who is an expert in the area you desire to know more about.

Be sure to hire a consultant who is accomplished in the field in which you seek knowledge.

CHAPTER TWENTY-NINE

Get Up With The Chickens

"The reward of a thing well done is having done it." —Ralph Waldo Emerson

My grandparents had a little farm in Connecticut. They got up early and did their chores and had lots of free time toward the end of the day. They were happy and successful. People ask them how they did it. My grandmother would simply answer, "I get up with the chickens."

When you have a dream and are bombarded and distracted by outside influences, here's a little secret. Set your alarm clock one hour earlier than usual and get up with the chickens. This will give you that all-important 'me' time everyday to do something a little extra for yourself.

You can sit around expecting a windfall to land into your lap; however, you have read many times before that you have to get into action to make things happen. My grandmother also used to say (in Italian), "patience and poverty are sisters." In other words, you can't release it to the Universe so much so that you literally do nothing to make your dreams happen. You can't be so passive that you become poor. That would be a sin and a waste of life. So, get up and into action early in the day. Get up with the chickens.

Like Benjamin Franklin said, "Early to bed, early to rise, makes a man healthy, wealthy and wise." That's a good Big Picture method for being a successful artist.

Chapter Twenty-Nine's Studio Play Sheet

Set your clock one hour earlier for one month. This extra hour should be dedicated to your dream endeavor. This is quiet time just for you. Set clear boundaries and be sure to tell others not to disturb you during your quiet time. Use this time to read, research, dream, envision, meditate and create your action plan for success.

During the same month period, go to bed one-half hour earlier than usual to get proper rest and relaxation. Be well rested.

When you're well rested, you make better sales.

CHAPTER THIRTY

Find a Niche You Can Scratch

"If we knew what it was we were doing, it would not be called research, would it?" —Albert Einstein

You hear this all the time: Location, Location, Location, but what does that mean when making a living with your art? Here is what that means in art sales.

Know your market – and its location

Know your niche- and its location

Know your customer – and their location

Know your attitude – and its location

Do your market research

You can't expect to make money selling the wrong product to the wrong folks, in the wrong place. However, you can expect to make money selling the right stuff to the right folks in the right place!

People are always searching for what they want and very often, they find it. Sometimes, people search for what they want and never find it.

We often hear statements like this at the gallery. "I went everywhere trying to find this, wow! I wish I had known you were here earlier!" Then, we hear this. "I knew I'd find you here! What a perfect place for your gallery."

I found my niche market! That place where I can focus and thrive with my art. You must find your niche market as well and it may very well be right in front of you.

Once you find it, it will be tempting to work like crazy; however, do not spread yourself too thin. You'll burn out by trying to be everywhere at once. It makes your art sloppy. We've all seen businesses that try to grow too fast and then disappear overnight. Solve other people's problems with something you know how to create with your art niche. This may be in your very own back yard. There's nothing wrong with being a big fish in a small pond.

Being of service in a niche and making art from your heart is powerful. Feed your mind with abundant gratitude; you have the ability to serve others with your talents. Look for good local opportunities that up build your experiences and enhance faith in your success ability. Always act quickly. Opportunity sometimes comes in failures, setbacks, and letdowns. When experiencing such things, ask yourself empowering question such as, *What is the best way I can do this?* Let that gel and let it go. Perhaps there is a way to do it; perhaps there is not. Don't get stuck in endless analyzing; pick up the positive vibes and get moving. Many people find their successes after big belly flops in life.

There are some things only you can do and there are some things you shouldn't do. Let the experts assist you. I see artists hanging onto control so tightly when trying to get their art out there that they are suffocating and extinguishing their careers.

Start locally. A friend, Michelle Robinson, operates a high-end framing store in my city. One day, we were talking about recycling in our stores. She had a lot of extra moldings and glass left over from finished jobs and didn't want to throw them away, adding more to landfills. There wasn't enough of any of the materials to frame a regular large-size picture, but I had several small pictures that were unsold that I thought would look fabulous as framed miniature-size pictures. We teamed up; I created small prints of my art and Michelle framed them lavishly. I took them to the gallery and sold them, split the profits with her and laughed all the way to the bank. Something that almost went to the dumpster turned out to be a profit because two experts teamed up to create a new product.

Use the resources and powers that be that are already set in place and apply them to your business plan.

If you're a painter, let a framer mat and frame your art, let a printer make your prints and find a vendor who does all three as well. The more steps you can eliminate, the more you can concentrate on making your art and getting it out there. If you're a writer, you probably wouldn't plant a forest, harvest the wood to make the paper, figure out how to turn the wood into paper and then set up a printing factory to get your writings into a book, would you? No; there are systems in place to help you do that.

There are plenty of naysayers, controllers and critics out there if you need or like to procrastinate. Critics who claim something can't be done are a dime a dozen. They will never go away, so get over it. Your own opinion builds your reality. Never give that power to someone else. Never give your power to procrastination either!

Creative Activity Points

Find your niche. STAY FOCUSED. Do one thing that you do great, not twenty different things you do well. Find your niche.

Within a niche, there is an infinite supply of abundance. Develop your niche customer and tailor a system to bring them your art efficiently and productively.

Replicate what other business experts have done in niche markets and apply their expertise with your own twist to your art process.

Don't physically or mentally waste time when an expert can do it for less money and in less time.

Stick to what you do best and let others with the proper tools help you achieve your Big Picture.

Don't give your art away foolishly. Learn how to get your art correctly licensed and copyrighted; get your art on products and responsibly create many sources of income.

Team up with other vendors and create new income by joining forces.

Efficiency and joined forces saves the planet from creating extra waste.

CHAPTER THIRTY-ONE

Be a Doorway

*"How can I be useful? Of what service can I be?
There is something inside me; what can it be?"* —Vincent Van Gogh

Almost every day at my studio I am asked ,"Do you paint from memory, real life or photographs?" I am a studio painter ,so it is rare for me to paint live outdoors. When I am in the studio, I work from photographs I have taken out in the field and while it is rare for me to paint outdoors, I do like to sketch out in nature. Sometimes I work from inspiring photos that friends give me too. There are times, however, when I do paint from memories or more often I like to say "from the future" things I see in my artist mind's eye or daydreams. At times, things may happen later in time and I look back at the painting and think, *Well that is just uncanny; how could I have seen this experience before it happened? Now where the heck did that come from?* Are our gifts more than artistic? Painting the future can be quite powerful and unsettling, as well as exciting at times.

Many years ago while living in Connecticut, I drew a rendering of a Spanish style hacienda building, sort of like drawing of one's dream house. The odd thing (and who knows why) was that I drew my name on the side of the building, sort of like business signage. The odder thing was that some twenty years later, my gallery would be located in a building just like that in San Diego, California. One day while arriving to open up the shop for business, I was pleasantly surprised to find that my landlord had painted my name on the side of the building. Whether that means anything or not, it was a powerful affirmation (or message that manifested from a thought to a sketch and into reality from drawing the future). There can be different ways that messages come through in the art.

Another time this happened was very different; it had nothing to do with what I wanted to manifest and was more of just a message that came through my art expression. I was awarded an art exhibit in September of 2000 in New York City at the Leslie-Lohman Museum of Gay and Lesbian Art in SOHO in their **Painting Invitational**. I was one of just a handful of highly talented artists honored and selected for the exhibit. Daydreaming about the future and going to New York, I began painting at my San Diego home. I was not thinking about anything in particular about my art or manifesting anything other than daydreaming about going to the city. I lost all sense of time and felt as though I was not painting but was being painted through, and a cityscape with a fiery sunset, seen through a jaggedly shaped building, emerged. When I finished the canvas, it was dark outside. Where did the time go? I guess that is what artist's call being in the zone. When I looked at the picture, there were no strong feelings one way or the other about the image in the paint. I just found it odd and different from the style I normally created. Since I didn't care for it much and almost painted over it the next day, I stored it away with other pictures in my garage and forgot about it. With my art ready and pre-selected by the gallery, I began the task of getting it ready for shipment.

The time came for the selected art pieces to be shipped off for exhibition. Shortly thereafter, I traveled back to the east coast myself to see the art show hanging up at the opening and meet the other artists. It was exciting for me and besides, this would be close enough for my friends and family in the northeast to come to one of my art openings. When I first arrived and met with the gallery director the day before the opening, I remember it was a beautiful day like those fabulous days we get in Southern California so often. It was a very relaxed and informal meeting; I felt welcomed and at home; everything was taken care of and there were no worries on my plate. As with all true professional galleries, the wonderful staff made me feel completely relaxed. All I had to do was show up the next day. Being that it was such a spectacular end to a summer day, I decided to take a walk from SOHO to the World Trade Center after my gallery meeting. It would be perfect to go to the top of the building and see the marvelous views, and if it was clear enough, you could see four states from up there.

As I walked toward the enormous buildings, I was thrilled to be there, being a lover of architecture . New York is just the most exciting city to me. Having just landed a show in New York City, I literally felt like I was riding on top of the world; what a perfect way to celebrate it! Suddenly, as put my hand on the revolving door handle to enter the building, a strong feeling swooshed up from loudly within me, nudging me firmly from inside ,"NO! Go Away. Now.- RUN! " and I had a flash of something terrible. I felt very unsafe; my heart felt heavy and sad inside. I have always listened to that inner voice and stayed in the revolving door full circle and walked back out from the doors quickly, away from the building. As I walked away, I looked up and felt very unsettled and confused. Had I stepped into a doorway of another dimension? Was it a doorway for receiving some sort of information that I could not comprehend? It was very strange and I really wanted to go up to the observation deck. However, I paid attention to my gut feeling as it had served me well many times before in my life. *There will be another day to go up the tower*, I thought, *but not today.*

The art opening at Leslie Lohman was the very next day. It was a big success and full of all types of interesting people that I expected a New York show to have. I left feeling with a good sense of accomplishment. When I flew home from JFK International Airport to California a few days later, I snapped a photo of Manhattan from the window of the jet; it was the last time I saw the skyline of my favorite city intact. A year later to the very day I visited The World Trade Center was the attack on 911. Did the uneasiness I felt as I reached for the door mean anything? I'm not sure; many people have premonitions.

But, I found it odd that during a move in California, I pulled out that forgotten painting, which had been finished in 2002 and clearly saw it as the famous skeleton façade of the smoldering World Trade Center where I had stood exactly one year prior to the day of September 11, 2001.

The opening of The Painting Invitational was September 12, 2000. I would never trivialize the horrific events of that day; they certainly were not about me, but they jolted and upset me terribly, and made me think, *Had I painted the future?* I have read so many stories about people who should have be there that day and were not. Perhaps we are always tapped into some sort of informational level of understanding that we do not comprehend in the physical world we live in? It was a year away from an upcoming event yet I felt something wanted to protect me. Is time and space connected differently than we perceive? Could I have tapped into an aspect of time that was always present? Can we paint the future? Had my inner artist stepped in to tell me something about the future through what I painted and where I had visited? What did any of this mean? I am not sure, but I know that it has happened many times in my life. The results have all been different, not dire or tragic, but with many happy results too (some of which I have shared in this book). I believe those times including I tapped into a collective subconscious. But, this book is not my story; it's for helping you discover and pay attention to your divine artist blessings that you are tapped into and take them out of the shadows to thrive. Life is short and I believe we are prompted by artist spirit and angels to be used the best we can be with the abilities that we are given. Making a living with your art is much more than reaping financial rewards; it's about creating a new you. Living is life. I have come to realize for myself that living my SELF fully is a gift from somewhere I don't fully understand or comprehend with a human brain. However, I get to express this through art that others and I also enjoy. Do not waste your gifts; they may be the doorway for your spirit to grow.

At first, I wasn't sure how I felt about telling this story. Actually, I did not include this experience in the first printing of The Big Picture. I realized that if it happened to me, similar things may have happened to others and it's OKAY. If it could help someone relate to using their intuitive creativity, accept him or herself and see their own individual truth, it was time to share it.

The Big Questions

All this makes me wonder, *If we are we capable of painting the future through tapping into artistic phenomena, then could the artist's gift be more than meets the eye?* I believe yes, they are. *Could we own up to how powerful our creativity, divine inspiration, or seeing really is? Could we tap into far more than just another art piece we take for granted, which we could paint over or discard for not making sense? When the artist is in the zone, are they tapping into an unknown realm or source of information?* There may or may not be visual answers to my questions but I think they are well worth asking and exploring. If there is no answer I am comfortable with that. What I know is this: I believe there is much more to being a gifted artist than talent. I keep making my art and do not let informational anomalies distract or stop me from creating. They are part of the divine tools in my tool chest that God has given this artist. As the writer Emile Zola says, "The artist is nothing without the gift but the gift is nothing without the work."

I rarely take myself seriously; sometimes things that I think of or feel make no sense and moments pass, but I do take my art seriously and what inspirational gift comes through when it is created. Perhaps you may not relate to any of this; however, I urge you to be open to investigate your inner messages that may emerge from and through your art expression. I find they will come in when you are most relaxed. I know what happened to me after that experience and that is how my art evolved again, as did I, in a different direction. I owned up to how I had been given gifts to see things and how I was being intuitively inspired and that it was all good. My career has flourished. I am a firm believer that it is very important to own up to your artistic capabilities. They may be more divinely received than we let them on to be.

When you are daydreaming, relax, breathe and look into painting the future. Even if you do not paint or draw, try it; get a starter set of acrylic paints. Acrylics wash up easily with soap and water and they dry fast too. You can draw first with pencil and then color in the picture with the acrylics. It can be realistic or abstract. The important thing is that you daydream while you create. The art you make need not be bleak or scary; just go with the flow; if you do not want to paint, then write a story about it, breathing and relaxing to see what happens.

Your successful Big Picture is also every person's creation at the highest level of creativity.

People are going to want to know how you did it' how you became successful at creating your Big Picture. My advice is this-many people can hold the door open for you, but you alone have to walk through that doorway. Be a doorway, not a doormat. Honor and value your time and worth. Broadcast Inner Genius!

We all have to pay our dues; however, we also have to eat and take care of our responsibilities. We need to and can make a living with our art. One reason I started charging for my artist consulting services was because of the impolite behavior of those who lined up for free advice. Too often, these artists would step right in front of paying customers with no clue of how rude they were. I see this happening in other cities when I visit galleries. Don't do this. Make appointments before you enter someone else's place of business. If your visit is unannounced, it better be because you are there to buy something. Never just walk into a place of business and expect free advice from a professional artist or gallery owner; please inquire about the consultation fee. Would you walk into a medical professional's office and expect an on-the-spot exam for free? Of course not!

Yes, share business tips and advice; however, consider bartering (mentoring in exchange for your services). Most times, people don't act on free advice anyway because like the air we breathe, they take free for granted.

Perhaps you can offer a free talk with the purchase of your products or a paid talk and a free product. Remember, money is an exchange of appreciation energy. Be a success doorway, not a success doormat and you will gain respect and new customers. Give a free product of value; never discount your services.

Your Big Picture is never a finished product. A Big Successful Picture is all about the journey, the dreaming and the unfolding of what you build and what you do with it.

Don't let your greatness go unheard. There is a lot of unknown greatness that was never acted upon and it's everywhere, quiet and buried six feet under the ground. Don't waste your time on analyzing questions like, "What if I could have…..?" Or, "I wonder if I would have done this or that when I could have?" Again, change that type of question into an empowering statement such as, "The answer comes to me now with the best results."

Make a decision to check out your dreams and your inner brilliance, which is why you're here. Share that brilliance with others. Sadness based on regrets is a huge waste of time and energy. People will tell you, "NO, you can't do that" or, "Who are you to think you can do that?" The world has changed a lot and there are more opportunities than ever for you. Do those inner and outer voices still pop up? The voices feed on your ego and keep you held down. I want to assure you that there are people who depend on your dreams, and are waiting for you to shine and bring your brilliance forward into the light of the world.

People, some who are not even born yet, are praying for the answers that only you can give! How do I know this? Think about it. Most people alive today did not personally know Thomas Edison, Henry Ford, Alexander Graham Bell, Madame Currie or the Wright Brothers, and yet our lives have greatly benefitted from their dreams and ideas. These folks acted on their dreams and you can too. If you don't know what they did, study them; read up on the persons I have quoted in this book and you will be inspired. While they are responsible for many finished products we currently enjoy, their dreams continue to unfold in new ways for a future time they could not yet see. You're no different from them.

Once you make a decision to do what you want, the opposite will continue to show up. Don't worry; this is happening because now you are aware of it and now you can make choices about what you want and don't want to manifest in your life. The finest Big Picture is sometimes best measured in the smiles you receive and give, the laughs you share, and the hands you hold as opposed to what's in the bank account.

It's important to remember friends and family first. Sometimes, when things appear out of control, we can forget that. All that we've got is now; the past and future are really just artistic illusions. The miracle of the moment is what we're living, so live it with gusto! Enthusiasm creates the future you want! The time is always right to do and live right. It's the delight of the Big Picture moment right now that counts and it's a miracle, so enjoy it.

Putting labels on people is a terrible thing. The artist hates being labeled. Yet, oddly many artists label themselves as struggling, impoverished and plain old starving. It's time to change that. What is all that supposed to mean, anyway? Let's face it, struggle doesn't feel good.

Instead of taking miracles for granted, ask yourself, *what does that mean? Where did that come from?* There doesn't have to be a scientific or religious explanation to everything or anything; just ask yourself, *what does that mean?*

If God sent you a message, would you know how to receive it? Your creativity and the ability to use it is a miracle. It's your message from God. Talk to God, listen and spread your creative light.

Stop talking to your ego because it's confusing and makes you fearful. Its advice to you is- you will starve as an artist and go without. Ask the divine within for direction and listen with your artist spirit. Your artist spirit will always come from power and truth, not only to create your art but also your wealthy artist life. Acknowledge its truth and be free. When you do this, you spread the creative light and heal other artisans who witness the example of your brilliance.

The artist's light need not be dimmed or extinguished through the envious ego's fear and scare tactics. Don't be afraid to tell other artists and non-artists that you love their spirit or their creativity. Struggle doesn't feel good; it's a force that causes spiritual and physical illness. The myth of the starving artist has killed off many talented careers. Change this by speaking to others with love. Your light will nourish their spirit and help heal their experiences of doubt and inspire them. Everyone is an artist in some way and artists are natural healers. Be one.

Share your joy and good experiences; smile; thank people; wave at them and be generous, loving and friendly. Your healing power will spread your light and ignite theirs. As they heal, so do you. When you enjoy living with your artistry, you'll find it is who you really are and this will lead you to live exceptionally well in a prosperous place; your artist needs are met and you can thrive.

Creative Activity Points

Give a free product of value with purchase; never discount your services. You are making a living as an artist.

Love is free and the ultimate power in your life. Fall in love with your Big Picture; adore everything about it and share what you put in it; others will benefit as well.

Your business may attract many different things; choosing what to accept in life is yours alone. You have a choice not to accept something unwanted.

Be loving; family, friends and health all come first. The power of love trumps all.

Make appointments before you enter someone else's place of business unless you are there to purchase their product or service.

When asking for advice from a professional artist or gallery owner, be sure to ask about the consultation fee.

The cost of looking for a free ride creates a starving artist mentality.

In the words of Mark Twain, "Don't go around saying the world owes you a living. The world owes you nothing. It was here first."

Key Creative Points to Review

THE SEVEN CREATIVE STEPS AND STUDIOS

1. Step One: I Beckon Inner Genius. Take Ownership of the Big Picture. Make decisions by focusing on the solutions to your problems. Develop yourself the best you can with good study programs. Get moving into action with love.
2. Step Two: My Beliefs Influence Genius. You have a magical mind. Don't believe everything you think. Train your mind positively with clarity. Release false beliefs and slay the mythical starving artist dragon. Continuously create artistic prosperity with a thriving imagination that magnetizes your Big Picture.
3. Step Three: I Broadcast Inner Gratitude. Serve the world with gratitude, appreciation and kindness from your heart. Work with experts and focus on making the world a better place for yourself and others through your shared value and gained wisdom.
4. Step Four: I Build Interpersonal Growth. Tend to your relationships. Nurture healthy relationships and release unhealthy relationships with love. Laugh at your ego and surround yourself in harmony with love and support.
5. Step Five: Be In Grace. Relax and replenish, take care of your body, mind and artist spirit self. Enjoy knowing your deepest truest self and appreciate and value the fact that you are a living illuminated artist!

6. Step Six: Be Integrity Grounded. Find, investigate and live out your passions with fiscal, ethical and emotional responsibility. Follow your vision and map out your inspirations to make a contribution through valuable action.
7. Step Seven: Be a Business Information Gateway. Balanced action in self-investment combined with appreciation and gratitude is a nourishing magnet for success. Track, document, your physical and inspirational success. Share and appreciate with love your action successes every day for continuous inspiration.

Don't forget or let go of the artist that you were meant to be. Struggling is an option, just as focusing on positive and action-oriented thoughts can bring you right to the doorstep of your Big Picture. It's your choice…now decide to Broadcast Inner Genius!

I have had the honor of meeting and talking with some iconic artists who shared these important messages, which turned out to be the necessary pathway to finding myself as a true artist.

Anna Hyatt Huntington, from my hometown of Redding (Connecticut), taught me that art was important. Keith Haring, a young man full of passion, drive and symbolism showed me that we see things in pictures. Art historian, Aubrey Walter, told me that I was more than deserving to share my talent for art with the world through books, and Paul Cadmus, perhaps the greatest American figurative artist, spent an hour of his valuable time with me and told me to be courageous and that I was doing it right.

Our synchronistic paths crossed for a reason; your path is here right now. My hope is that this book is a doorway for you to discover your own good artistic travel.

So, what are you waiting for? The Universe has put out an Artist Call and you answered it. Get out of the studio and out into the awaiting world!

You know how to make your art. Learn how to love being a businessperson; love the technology that exists for you, the sites you see and the people you have met and have not yet met; let the experts help you! Tell those experts your story and show them your creations; let them fall in love with you and your art.

Create harmonious business relationships with clarity and intention. Make sure you resonate with these co-creators. It pays to be an artist!

Be the artist that you were born to be - right now - and draw the line! Make your new symbols; get into action. Now is the time to suit up and show up for the life of your dreams, or something better! Trust, believe and know your success as an artist. There's no day like today to do what you've been waiting to do for so long. You are pure unlimited potential and have all that you need, so get going! Your success has always been there, patiently waiting for you to find it. Feel good and embrace the biggest picture because it is your divine right. Things happen when you get in touch with your true inner artist self. Get moving on it!

Just as in art, the more that you explore any process or perspective and the more loving energy you put into it, the more benefits you will receive. Only you can shatter the starving artist story once and for all. Create a positive impact on the world and let your creative light shine.

May love, light and gratitude always go before you!

RD "Randy" Riccoboni

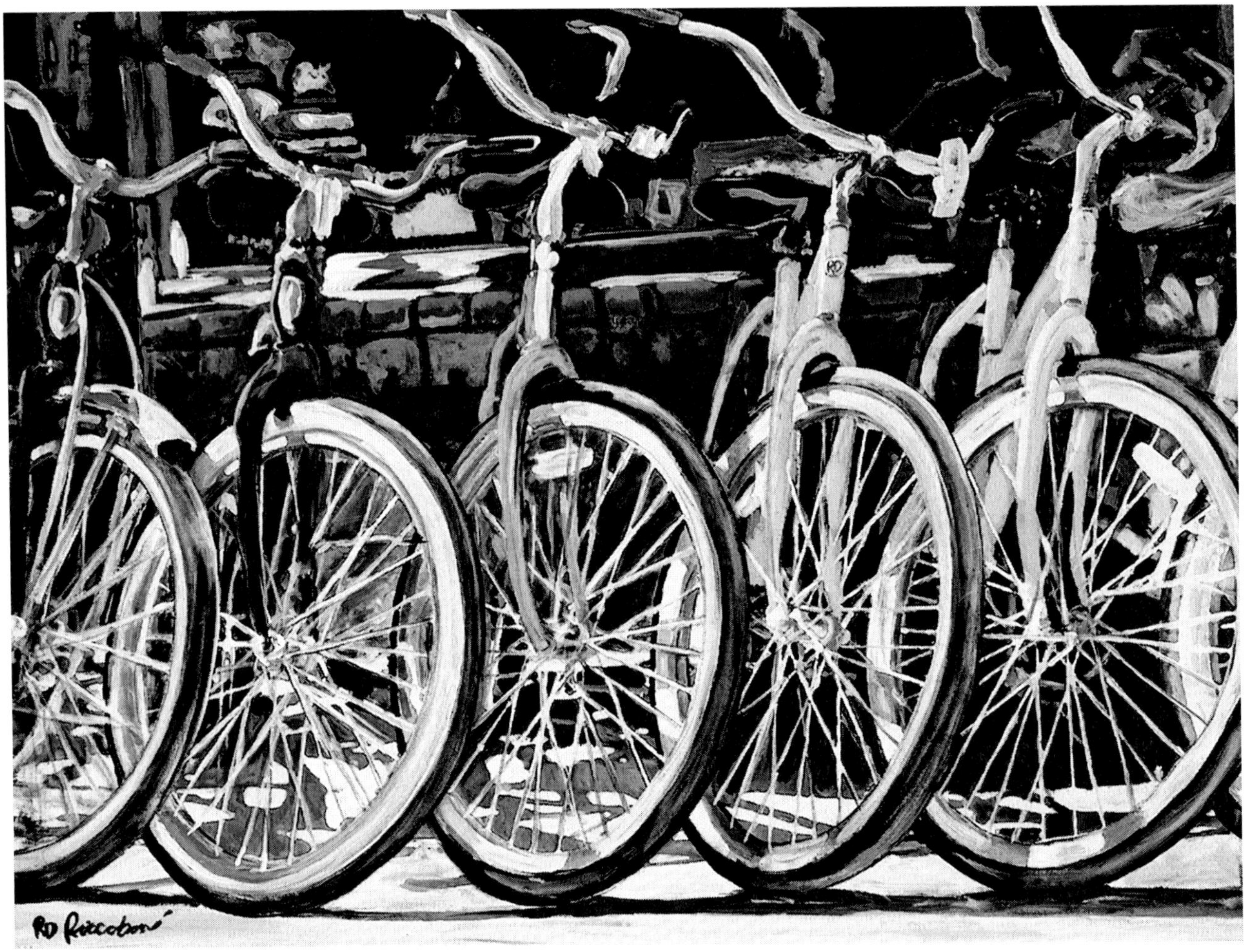
RD Riccoboni

About the Author

RD Riccoboni, Randy to his friends, is an innovative, self-taught artist who began painting at age four when he got into his mothers paint-by-numbers kit. Known as The California Artist who boldly paints spectacular landmarks in an exciting impressionistic style, happy colors are his trademark, and the results of his career have been astounding. The artist credits encouragement by family and teachers for his drive and inspiration, which has led the way to his success as a best-selling author, speaker and inspirational visionary. In 2007, RD moved his popular Beacon Artworks Gallery into the beautiful Fiesta de Reyes in Old Town's San Diego State Historic Park.

His paintings on canvas and paper depict everyday life experiences, travels, as well as places of local interest, including Balboa Park landmarks. RD's internationally recognized artwork represents community and a sense of place in a positive and life-affirming manner. A fan of architecture, RD is currently working on drawings and paintings of vanishing historic American buildings and landscape for his Art Traveler project.

Next time you're in Old Town, enjoy a visit to Beacon Artworks Gallery and meet RD Riccoboni in person, or visit http://beacon-artworks.com from the comfort of your home.

"What drives and inspires me is a passion for forward thinking. I pick up on the positive and beautiful vibrations of color, contrast, perspective and spirit that surround our daily lives. I create art and business of it with a mission that is trail-blazing for other artists and non-artists, alike. I hope my art work and writings trigger inspiration and happiness in you, whether you are the creator, the appreciator, or both and help you to create and make the world a better place, starting right in our own neighborhoods."

RD Riccoboni

Biographical Highlights

The Archives of the City of Los Angeles City Hall, Los Angeles California

University of California, Los Angeles, California

The Morris Kight – McCadden Place Collection University Southern California

California State University, Los Angeles California

San Francisco Public Library, San Francisco California

Los Angeles County Museum of Art, ARSG Los Angeles California

The White House, Washington DC   Office of The National AIDS Policy Coordinator

LAC + USC Medical Center Los Angeles California

Cultural Affairs Department of the City of Los Angeles

Barnsdall Art Park, Los Angeles California

Leslie Lohman Gay Art Foundation, New York, New York

Yale University, New Haven Connecticut

Historic Lafayette Hotel, San Diego, California

San Diego Art Institute, Museum of the Living Artist Balboa Park, San Diego, California

Beacon Artworks Gallery, San Diego, California

Old Town San Diego State Historic Park, San Diego, California

American Psychological Association- Washington DC

San Diego Convention Center San Diego, California

2012 Recipient - Making A Million Look Small Award of Excellence

Also by RD Riccoboni

***Books from Beacon Artworks Corporation,
1010 University Ave, Suite 474, San Diego, CA 92103***

Everyday Intentions, Art and Wisdom, RD Riccoboni and
Jayne Moffitt, - Beacon Artworks Corporation

RD Riccoboni, from Old Town to Newtown

RD Riccoboni Paintings and Drawings - Beacon Artworks Collection

My Positive Evidence Journal -Illustrations and Affirmations
from American artist RD Riccoboni

My Magnificent Evidence Journal - Affirmations from American artist RD Riccoboni

RD Riccoboni, The San Diego Paintings, Collector's Edition Volume 1

RD Riccoboni, Paintings, Collector's Edition Volume 2

My Balboa Park Art Book, Art from Mr. Riccoboni's studio
and gallery for you to color and have with.

My San Diego Art Book, Art from Mr. Riccoboni's studio and gallery

Books from: More Heart than Talent Publishing, Inc. Stockton Ca,92507

Manifest Success, the Ultimate Guide to Living the Life of
Your Dreams, Debbi Chambers 2008 Co-Author

Onrise Publications, Boise, Idaho 83702

Manifest Success Volume.2 Motivation, Momentum,
Miracles, Deborah L. Chambers 2010 Co-Author

Books from: Editions Aubrey Walter, London England

Rainbow Nation - Paintings from the Gay Community – Editions Aubrey Walter 1996

Making A Million Look Small – Stories To Inspire You
In Saying Yes To A Much Larger Life.

Illustrations and Art by RD Riccoboni

Cover
San Diego Sunset, 16 x 24 acrylic on canvas

Introduction
Arches at Griffith Park 16 x 20 acrylic on paper

Studio one
The Road to Torrey Pines, 8 x10 pen and ink drawing

Studio Two
Rollercoaster, 8 x10 pen and ink drawing

Studio Three
Torrey Pine Tree, 8 x10 pen and ink drawing

Studio Four
Arbor Colonnade Balboa Park San Diego, 8 x10 pen and ink drawing

Studio Five
Point Loma Lighthouse, 8 x8 pen and ink drawing

Studio Six
Cliff Walk La Jolla, 8 x 10 pen and ink drawing

Studio Seven
Crossing The Bridge, Balboa Park San Diego, 8 x 10 pen and ink drawing

Bicycles in A Row
24 x 30 Acrylic on Canvas

Resources

As the business world changes, new companies that can help your business emerge daily while others go away. Be sure to do web searches by keyword and always ask for referrals for your best results.

Business Plan

Writing a Convincing Business Plan by Arthur R. DeThomas and Lin Grensing-Pophal from Barron's Business Library. http://www.barronseduc.com

Publishing

Publishing Unleashed: http://publishingunleashed.com/

Book Design and Editing Services

Integrative Ink: http://www.integrativeink.com

Self Publishing

www.lulu.com
www.createspace.com
www.iuniverse.com/packages
www.xlibris.com
www.outskirtspress.com

Quick Response Codes (QR Codes)

http://www1.instantcustomer.com
http://phonescanvideo.com
http://qrcode.kaywa.com/

Postcards Business Cards, Greeting Cards, Posters

http://gotprint.net/g/welcome.do
http://vistaprint.com
http://www.modernpostcard.com

Art Printing – Giclee

http://imagekind.com
http://canvasondemand.com

Putting your art on various products

http://cafepress.com
http://www.zazzle.com

Photographing fine art

www.w9imaging.com

Custom Framing

www.raystreetcustomframing.com/

Online Business Expert Peggy McColl

http://www.destinies.com

Important Social Media sites

www.facebook.com
www.linkedin.com
www.twitter.com
www.youtube.com

To register your art/book copyright

If you live in the U.S. www.copyright.gov
If you live in Canada www.cb.-cda.gc.ca/info/registration-e.html
If you live in Australia www.copyright.org.au
If you live in the UK www.copyrightservice.co.uk

Sites that will help you with website hosting and design

www.fatcow.com
www.smallbusiness.yahoo.com
www.networksolutions.com
www.godaddy.com
www.intuit.com